Lyman Allen

Political Problems

Essays on Questions of the Day

Lyman Allen

Political Problems
Essays on Questions of the Day

ISBN/EAN: 9783337073404

Printed in Europe, USA, Canada, Australia, Japan

Cover: Foto ©Suzi / pixelio.de

More available books at **www.hansebooks.com**

POLITICAL PROBLEMS

★

Essays on Questions of the Day

★

BY

LYMAN ALLEN, M. D.

AUTHOR OF "FRUIT GROWING IN SOUTHERN CALIFORNIA" IN "A SOUTHERN
CALIFORNIA PARADISE" ETC.

SAN FRANCISCO
CALIFORNIAN PUBLISHING CO.
1892

PREFACE

∴

There obtains in the minds of a large and increasing number of people, a conviction that we fall far short of living by the full light of modern knowledge and experience ; that the masses of the people do not receive an equitable share of the fruits of their labor, and do not enjoy an adequate measure of benefit from the cumulated results of human labor, study, research and invention ; that in a land of abundant wealth and production there should not be such want, such privation and such necessity for unremitting toil ; that somehow and somewhere there must be grave errors in our system of society, in our commercial life or in our government, much waste and loss and injustice, to cause the wide difference in condition between the many who toil through life for a bare living, and the few who are possessed with abundant wealth.

It is a common error with physicians to attribute a patient's sickness to some one cause, and to treat the case accordingly, when, perhaps, there are several causes for his ailment, and it is not unusual for some of those who seek to enlighten us upon the causes of our financial ills to ascribe them all to some one cause, and to propose some one remedy as a complete cure for poverty and for all our material disorders.

It is the purpose of this work to consider the various principal causes for our financial ailments ; to show the relative importance of each ; to point out the defects in some of the proposed remedies for these disorders ; and to advocate such remedies as appear, in the light of reason or experience, to offer the largest measure of relief to the burdened industrial classes.

LYMAN ALLEN.

PASADENA, CALIFORNIA,
December, 1892.

CONTENTS

PART I

OBSTACLES, DIFFICULTIES AND DUST

PART II

A SEARCH FOR CAUSES OF POVERTY AND THE UNEQUAL DISTRIBUTION OF WEALTH

PART III

REMEDIES FOR DEFECTIVE GOVERNMENT, FOR FAULTY EDUCATION, FOR SOCIAL EVILS, FOR BURDENS OF OPPRESSIVE MONOPOLIES AND INEQUITABLE TAXES, AND FOR UNEQUAL DISTRIBUTION AND WASTE OF WEALTH.

PART IV

AFTERMATH—RESULTS AND LESSONS OF THE CAMPAIGN OF 1892—THE POLITICAL OUTLOOK

POLITICAL PROBLEMS

⚬

PART I

⚬

OBSTACLES, DIFFICULTIES, AND DUST

POLITICAL PROBLEMS

✛

CHAPTER I.

✛

PARTY PREJUDICE—POPULAR PREJUDICE

At the outset of any effort to reform our methods of government or to improve the condition of the people, we are confronted by a mountain of party prejudice. This consists of—1, the conviction that one's party contains nearly all the good people, and that the other party is largely composed of the worst elements of society; 2, that upon the success of one's party depends the welfare and perpetuity of all good government; 3, that fealty to one's party, to its every measure and every candidate, is the first duty of every good citizen, and that one who fails to support his party is a bolter and a traitor; 4, that loyalty and patriotism mean subservience to party dictates; 5, that whatever the party papers and speakers say *must* be true, and *goes*; 6, that duty to family, to church, to society, to the country are second to duty to party.

Partisan prejudice leads to submission to *party tyranny.* It becomes the whip and the club by which good men are forced to submit to the dictates of the party bosses; by which the man who hates the saloon is compelled to vote and work in its interest, and by which a man who abhors **iniquity** and despises a corrupt man is made to march up to the polls and cast a ballot for men he knows are corrupt, and who may vote or work for such schemes as they are paid to work for, though they be subversive of all good government and wasteful of the people's wealth.

Party prejudice apologizes for that great enemy of all good and efficient government, the " spoils system." It blinds men's eyes to the corruption which exists and largely controls party management. As the old, time serving parties could no longer exist without party prejudice and party spirit, it becomes the chief duty of the party papers and leaders to strengthen and intensify them. In this way they are able to hold the party ranks together, to strengthen their outposts and entrench themselves against all raids and incursions. In short party prejudice is the one great obstacle in the way of success of all attempts by the people to undertake reforms in our government. It makes it nearly impossible to get a hearing for any cause which is not advocated as a party measure, or to get any full or just consideration of it when once heard.

Anything, a thunderbolt from heaven or a tidal wave from the deep sea! a Farmers' Alliance or a cry for cheap money, which would knock this abominable conceit out of the heads of several millions of good American citizens, and leave them in a condition to consider the things which vitally concern their temporal salvation, would be as the first glimmer in the east which hails the coming day !

POPULAR PREJUDICE—"THE GOOD OLD WAY"

In all ages men have opposed improvements and reforms. In science, in inventions, in politics and in religion this has been true. Men have been persecuted, imprisoned or executed for announcing the discovery of a great law of nature, for trying to introduce a labor-saving machine, for promulgating a new religious doctrine, or for advocating a social or moral reform.

This was true one thousand or one hundred years ago, and it is in a measure true today. We do not need to go back one hundred years or ten years to search for a hero or a martyr. Not only Galileo, and Latimer, and Williams, and Lovejoy and their compeers, but Gambrel and Haddock add to the long list of martyrs.

We should be slow to ridicule or denounce any one without due consideration, for advocating some new method or plan for improving the physical, the material, the social or moral condition of mankind, simply because it strikes us as being absurd or unwise.

We are accustomed to accept our present ways and methods as being the best that can be devised, and to consider every innovation as wild and visionary. Men prefer ·what they are pleased to think is the "good old way." If potatoes have been "planted in the dark of the moon," dark of the moon it is! As unregenerate infants were held to be eternally damned, damned they must be! As woman's "sphere" was circumscribed to the home, home she must stay! As Latin was the chief study in a liberal course fifty years ago, so it must be to-day. And as there are tens of thousands of democrats

and republicans who feel that they must live and die in
the fold of the good old party, it may be necessary to
wait until many of them pass on before we shall see the
fullness of the better day. (A good Methodist Bishop
remarked that "there could be a union between the
church North and South as soon as we had a few prominent funerals.")

CHAPTER II

POLITICAL IGNORANCE—DEFECTIVE SOURCES OF KNOWLEDGE

The ordinary citizen depends almost wholly for his
knowledge, his facts, his news and his opinions upon all
subjects relative to political and governmental affairs
(and this includes many moral and social questions
which should be treated by the government), upon his
party paper. The party paper as a rule publishes such
facts and statements as are in the interests of its party
(or derogatory to the interests of the other parties), and
suppresses all facts which are not in its interest. This
is what it was born for, and what the party bosses hire it
to do.

How can a man correctly judge who does not have the
facts on which to base a correct judgment? How can we
expect the ordinary American citizen, well educated
though he be, to accept or even consider any plan
or idea of reform in government which is opposed

by his party, and either ignored, ridiculed or denounced by the party papers, while he depends on such papers for facts and conclusions in regard to it?

If popular government has not perished from off the face of the earth, popular knowledge of government and the subjects which should be treated by the government have almost disappeared so far as the teachings of the American party paper is concerned. It is a *conspiracy of misrepresentation and silence.*

These statements will not be accepted by the ordinary citizen who is solid for his party. Even men and women who are well informed in a general way, flatter themselves that their daily paper furnishes them all the news of the day which is of any moment to a substantial citizen. Their daily paper is loaded with news. It is a great blanket sheet. The managers represent the very soul of enterprise. The paper gives full particulars of all obtainable cases of scandal, and if there is a dearth of such news it has some stories of that class made to order! It gives full page accounts of divorce trials! It publishes lengthy reports of the "rounds" of the prize ring! It contains many other things of a similar character which go to make it a great engine for the depression of the social and moral conditions of humanity.

And then it has the associated press dispatches, and "you know" that these dispatches contain all the political news of any importance to any body, (to the old parties, would be correct.) Who originated the press dispatches? Who manage them? Who use them? Who pay for them? Why the associated press of course. Who are they? The leading daily papers, nearly all of which uphold one or other of the old parties. No body else. That is to say, they are managed *in the interest* of those w^o pay for them. It is a matter of business with them. They gather such news as they are called upon to furnish.

The press dispatches contain such news as are not prejudicial to either old party, to whose organs they are sent. The faults, the failings, the lapses from rectitude of the party leaders, must as a rule be passed in silence. No stained garments must be exposed to the public. No evil practices may be criticised. No unwelcome reforms favored.

Each old party depends upon spoils, upon plunder, upon the saloon, upon the great monopolies and trusts, upon rings and bosses, upon bribers, brewers, saloon-keepers. And these great agencies and agents necessary for party power must not be derided, and the press reporters must hew to this line.

For example, whoever read in a republican paper anything about the notorious Gas Trust of Philadelphia, a ring as bold, as corrupt, as grasping as the celebrated Tweed Ring of New York? This Gas Ring held complete sway in Philadelphia for about twenty years—from 1860 to 1881—fattened upon the people, controlled the republican party of the state and in this way almost absolutely ruled the state. It also had large influence in national affairs. Mr. James Bryce in his "American Commonwealth," says of the ring:

"The possession of the great city offices gave the members of the ring the means not only of making their own fortunes, but of amassing a large reserve fund to be used for "campaign purposes." Many of these officers were paid by fees and not by salary. Five

officers were at one time in the receipt of an aggregate of
$223,000 a year or an average of $44,600 each. One, the
collector of delinquent taxes, received nearly $200,000 a
year. Many others had the opportunity, by giving out
contracts for public works on which they received large
commissions, of enriching themselves almost without
limit, because there was practically no investigation of
their accounts."

During the rule of the ring, from 1860 to 1881, the
city debt rose from $20,000,000 to $70,000,000, and taxation reached a point where it amounted to between one
fourth and one third of the net income from the property,
with the property assessed at nearly its full value.

This ring was finally broken through the exertions
of a Citizens' Committee of One Hundred. A reform
democrat, Mr. Hunter, was elected Mayor in 1881, and
the way for reform was opened. For a time many
reforms were instituted, corruption in high places was
stopped, bad laws repealed, and city politics purified.
But the labors of the Committee of One Hundred had
been so arduous, it took so much of their time, and they
were fought so persistently by the party leaders, that
the members became tired, and in 1883 and 1884, their
candidates were beaten by the republican machine, and
they retired from the field. (Any one wishing an account
of this ring should read Mr. Bryce's Work.) "As a dog
returneth to his vomit, and a sow that was washed to
her wallowing in the mire," so do the people in this
"land of the free and home of the brave" under the
blind dictation of party prejudice and party spirit return
to be led and robbed by party bosses.

After the Committee gave up its work, under machine
and ring rule the affairs of the city gradually returned

into some of the old ways, until it was again checked by
the revolt of a portion of the republican party of the
state from the notoriously corrupt management of the
party bosses, by the election of a democratic governor
in a state overwhelmingly republican, and finally by the
arrest of several offenders and the collapse of the Key-
stone Bank.

And the worst feature in connection with it is that
Mat. S. Quay, one of the most corrupt of all party
bosses, for years the boss of the republican machine in
Pennsylvania, was for a long time Chairman of the
National Republican Committee, and was kept in that
position for months after he had been publicly charged
with malfeasance in office, and until he was really compelled to resign by the clamors against him in his party
at home. And when he resigned his position as chairman, the committee "gave him a character," highly
commending him as a pure, high minded and patriotic
citizen!!

Now, such facts are not advertised in republican papers.
Of course the fact of Bardsley's arrest and defalcation
was mentioned in the press dispatches. When a public
officer is convicted of embezzlement the fact is made
public. But the facts connected with it and which led
up to it are not enlarged upon by a party paper.

On the other hand, the present notoriously corrupt management of New York City affairs under Tammany rule,
notwithstanding the fact that the ring was broken and the
offenders brought to justice during the noted Tweed administration, is not dwelt upon by democratic papers. Nor do
the democratic papers have anything to say about the
democratic ring which rules the city of Baltimore.

One of the most common cases of failure to give news by the great dailies is the obliviousness to news favorable to temperance and prohibition movements. Any one familiar with the facts knows this to be true. A marked instance of this was the failure of all the dailies to make any mention of the intimidation and violence practiced at the polls in the election in Omaha at the close of the prohibitory amendment campaign. There never was a case of the "shotgun policy" practiced in the South to intimidate the blacks from voting, more outrageous than was this case of " bludgeon policy " as practiced in Omaha on that day. There were many instances of intimidation, of men being hooted at, driven from the polls and beaten, on that day, in order to carry the election in the interest of the saloons and the old parties, but never a word appeared in regard to it in a single great daily, and not a mention of it in any associated press dispatch. The kind of press dispatches we saw at that time were: " Prohibition snowed under in Nebraska." " A big majority against the amendment." " Reports from Iowa go to show that Prohibition is losing ground there, and that the law will probably be repealed at the next session of the legislature." " Prohibition in Kansas is proving to be an utter failure; liquors are freely and openly sold everywhere in that state."

While the results of the State elections of 1891 were being reported, telegraph dispatches were sent over the country to the effect that the vote of the Farmers' Alliance had greatly fallen off, that the Alliance was evidently going to pieces and need no longer be feared as a disturbing element in politics. These reports were entirely without foundation. Although the total vote in

1891 was much less than that of 1890, there was uniformly an increase in the Alliance vote. In Kansas this increase was about 11 per cent. The Republican majority in South Dakota was reduced from 10,000 in 1890 to 2,760 in 1891, and in Nebraska the People's party came within 3,000 votes of defeating the combined power of both the old parties, and elected eleven district judges.

The same plan of either misrepresenting or entirely ignoring the facts, which had been practiced so long in regard to the Prohibition party, was thus begun with the People's party, and this system of lying by wholesale may be depended upon from the corrupt management of the old parties.

These reports were sent for political effect. No effort was made to correct them. In 1890 the Democratic party, in strongly Republican districts, united with the Alliance, but in 1891 in many localities the old parties combined in self defense against their common enemy.

Instead of this being a government *of* the people, *for* the people and *by* the people, it is a government *of* the party, *for* the party and *by* " the boss." The question with the modern statesman is not " What will benefit the people?" but " What will profit my party?" and " What will help me and my friends to a place?"

This chapter was written before the opening of the campaign of 1892, and it is but fair to say that there has been a decided improvement in the tone of many of the leading dailies this year in reporting news of the new parties. The reports of their conventions have been quite full and fair as compared with those of previous years. This is very commendable, and a notable sign of the times.

CHAPTER III

"THE SPOILS SYSTEM"—SALOON DOMINATION— WRONG IDEA OF GOVERNMENT

"The Spoils System" is responsible for nearly all of our present corrupt or inefficient administration of the government. Men get responsible positions in charge of the business and affairs of the nation, not because of fitness for the positions, not because they are honest, honorable, able, qualified and adapted to the places; but because of party service, because of "claims upon the party" or the party bosses, and because of ability and disposition to still serve the party, while occupying (not filling) a place in government employ.

In this way the party "boss," the men who manage the canvas, those who contribute the funds, the men who control the saloon vote, the bribers, the brewers, the "ward heelers," the thugs and the toughs are coming to a considerable extent to fill the offices from United States senator to policeman.

This is especially the case in the government of some of the large cities, and the power they obtain in the councils of the State and Nation, brings discredit and dishonor upon our public affairs and upon the name of popular government. The government of the average American city has come to be a disgrace and a blot upon our boasted civilization. Modern politicians deem the offices to be their legitimate spoils, and the people's wealth their legitimate plunder. This is the crying evil

19

and abomination of our politics and government to-day.
It is at once the life of the old, time serving parties, and
the death of decent popular government.

The mismanagement, extravagance and peculation too
often found in our administration of public affairs, and
for which the spoils system is responsible, is the chief
argument advanced in opposition to any proposed extension of public business by the government. We are told
that the government should not undertake more business
because there would be "so much corruption." This
argument comes from those who are defenders of the
spoils system, or from those who have lost faith in our
ability to carry on a pure and honest government, and is
in itself a charge that popular government in our great
Republic has already proved a failure.

*No reform of government can be effectually carried out
without complete and absolute reform of our civil service.*

SALOON DOMINATION

Next to the spoils system and going hand in hand with
it, comes the saloon, as a prime factor in American
politics. It is not simply the fact that the saloon is a
"school of vice" and a "nursery of crime" that makes
it an obstacle to any and all reforms, but the fact that in
our country it has in a measure come to dominate politics, and to shape legislation and select the officials, that
makes it an arch enemy to all good government.

Neither of the old parties, as a national party, has any
quarrel with the saloon. They both receive its support
and give it their countenance and endorsement. They
can not do otherwise and do not propose to.

It is true that in Iowa and to a less extent in Kansas the Republican party supports prohibition. The Republican State Convention in Iowa in 1891 pronounced by a vote of nine hundred and fifty one to one hundred and seven in favor of prohibition as the law of the state and against high license and local option. (This was written before the meeting of Iowa republicans of this year, at which their action was not nearly so pronounced for prohibition.)

It is also true that in several southern states a large part of the territory is under local prohibition and that in every case this has been brought about almost entirely by democratic votes. But these facts do not alter the general fact that in most of the northern and in all of the southern states, and as a national party, the Republican party is a license and a whiskey party; and that the Democratic party in all the northern states and as a national party is entirely devoted to the saloon interest so far as that is concerned.

The saloon is the friend of bribery and corruption; the copartner with the lottery, the gaming table and the bawdy house; the patron of the prize ring; the rendezvous of the burglar and the assassin; the headquarters of the "ward heeler" and the "thug," and the potent ally of the political boss. It is often the chosen place for the ward caucus and the precinct election. From no man or set of men can we expect any genuine, effective, or lasting service for reform who do not openly and boldly oppose this gigantic evil.

WRONG IDEA OF GOVERNMENT

Finally in considering state and national affairs, we must correct our ideas, rather our *sense* than our knowledge, of government; what it is; what it means. We should constantly bear in mind, that the *people are the rulers*. That we are or should be the government. That all power and authority is in us if we would but exercise it. That the officers of the government are *our servants*. We should instruct them.

All the money and support comes from us. The public lands are ours. The Government mortgages against the Union and Central Pacific Railroads are ours. All needless expense and waste and loss in public affairs comes out of our pockets. The nation has no bank, or mine, or considerable source of wealth except in the toil, the economy, the thrift and the wealth of its people. Every subsidy, every bounty, every pension, every tax, every expense *must be paid by our labor* or taken from our capital.

Let us not make the mistake of looking upon the government as something separate and apart from us, a thing in and of itself, depending on its own power, volition and resources. We should do nothing as a nation that we would not in like circumstances, do as individuals.

And we should always remember, that when we speak of the government, we speak of ourselves, our delegates, our servants and employes. So if there is praise or blame to bestow we are its recipients. Let us then profit by our experience and by that of others, even though we learn of the "pauper laborers" and "effete monarchies" of Europe, and of the despised heathen in far off isles of the sea. Let us not be vain of our wisdom or proud of our ways. We have much to learn, much to be ashamed of, much room for improvement.

Let us try to approach the subject with a clear vision and an honest mind, unclouded by party spirit, by old time prejudice or misrepresentation, and undisturbed by the clamor of those who would resort to desperate means or the ridicule of those who are well satisfied with present conditions.

Thus as we enumerate and specify these various obstacles which stand as a high wall in the way of material, social and moral advancement, we begin to realize in a measure how difficult it is to get a hearing for any cause or any method which does not accord with present ways, or cannot be worked out with the present political machines. We see how ignorant, how blind, and how deaf and dumb are the masses of the people to some of their best interests. We see how strong is the grip of the party, the "boss" and "the machine" and of the plutocrat, the spoilsman and the saloon.

TARIFF AS A SUPREME ISSUE

Lastly, we have the tariff question as the main issue between the old parties, monopolizing the thought of the people, preventing consideration of other questions, and acting as a cloud of dust, filling the eyes and distracting the attention of a majority of the American people. For particulars see chapter on the tariff.

PART II.

✦

A SEARCH FOR CAUSES OF POVERTY AND
THE UNEQUAL DISTRIBUTION
OF WEALTH

CHAPTER IV

MILLIONAIRES

At the outset of our consideration of the questions pertaining to the disparity in the material conditions of the people, and the causes for this disparity, we will observe first men of greatest wealth and the sources from which their vast accumulations have been derived, and perhaps in taking this general survey we may be able to learn some of the causes of poverty by observing the sources of greatest individual wealth. When too much of the life current flows to the central organs of the body the extremities become cold, and the patient has a chill. In like manner we may reasonably expect that when a large proportion of wealth—the life current of the nation—flows into the coffers of the few, the many must needs be impoverished by the drain upon the common source of supply. With the nation as with the individual, congestion at one point produces lack of blood at another.

Reliable information regarding the number of millionaires, and especially the amount and sources of individual wealth, are not readily obtainable. A statement of the amount of wealth of any of our great millionaires should be taken as approximate. We have, as a rule, no means of ascertaining with exactness the wealth of rich men in the United States, except after their death. In England, where an income tax is collected from the rich, it becomes the business of the government to know the

wealth of individuals. But we may learn the amount of
the wealth of our rich men with sufficient accuracy for
our comparisons.

Mr. Thomas G. Shearman, in his *Forum* article has made
an extended enumeration of some of our great millionaires
with an estimate of their individual wealth, which is
probably as nearly correct as may be found. The *New
York Tribune* has also furnished an extended list of men
throughout the country who are reputed to be worth a
million or more, but it does not give estimates of individual wealth, except in a few instances, so that its list is
not satisfactory in this respect. There is a wide difference
between a fortune of a million and one of a hundred
millions.

A notable fact in regard to millionaires is that the
United States has furnished, during the last thirty years,
a field for the accumulation of large fortunes vastly
beyond that of any other nation or of any other period in
history. Indeed, in that time individual fortunes have
been amassed in the United States upon such a stupend-
ous scale as to very far surpass any acquisition of wealth
before known among men.

England is the great commercial and financial center
of the business world, yet England, with her landed
nobility who own vast estates, her great bankers, manufacturers and merchants, does not furnish millionaires to
compare with those of our country. The noted bankers
of England and France, whose names are familiar to
American readers, do not nearly approach in the magnitude of their fortunes the colossal wealth of several rich
Americans.

During these three decades, while wealth has greatly

increased in the hands of the few, as a rule the values of
the farmers' lands, except in the newer states and in
proximity to cities, have depreciated, and the proportion
of farm mortgages and of tenant farmers has largely
increased. This would seem to indicate that the causes
which have made a few rich have made many poor. And
not this alone, but the fact that along with this rapid
accumulation of great fortunes we have an increase in
the proportion of people who lack for the comforts of life,
who are forced to the most exacting toil to maintain a bare
existence or are unable to find sufficient employment to
provide for a decent living ; that with our illimitable
sources and facilities for producing almost everything
required for the comfort of mankind there should be so
many who do not secure a fair share of the wealth produced, that is arresting the attention of the American
people and has incited the present upheaval in our political life.

With such notable and unquestionable facts, showing
the existence of conditions which have produced and are
still producing this wide inequality in the distribution of
wealth, we may well consider what the causes and what
shall be the remedies for these evils.

In our search for millionaires we will first look among
the farming classes, as they constitute the largest number
of workers and are the principal producers of wealth. Do
we find them ? Is there a considerable proportion of
farmers who have become millionaires? No. There is
not. We might search diligently and would find but few
instances of men who have made a million in any ordinary
farming enterprise. Men have made millions by securing
large tracts of cheap lands, especially of government

lands, by fraudulent entries or by collusion of dishonest government agents and holding for advanced values, by herding large flocks of cattle or sheep upon the public domain, and in some western states by growing grain upon an extended scale. Many farmers become " well to do," they acquire thousands, but not millions.

Who then are the millionaires, and how did they make their money ?   They are men who manage the railway and telegraph lines and express companies ; men who control the production and distribution of coal, and oil, lumber and refined sugar ; those engaged in manufactures of iron, steel, glass, cordage ; those engaged in mining silver, gold, copper and lead ; bankers, brokers, speculators ; those who have been made rich by rise of real estate in cities ; men who are in the position to dictate the prices people must pay for their meat and many other articles of prime necessity ; these and others who have to a large extent a monopoly of the business in which they are engaged, and are enabled to exact exorbitant charges for the services rendered the people.

By far the larger number of great American millionaires, and especially those . whose fortunes have been acquired during the last three decades, are men who have made their money mainly in constructing, capitalizing, manag - ing and consolidating railway lines.   Perhaps one-half of the total acquisition of the notably great fortunes in that time have been made in that way.   These are the men whose absorption of a large proportion of the profits of labor has been a chief cause for close times among so many people.

It is probable that a list of fifty individuals, includ- ing estates, could be made, whose combined wealth would aggregate $1,500,000,000, mainly amassed in railroad affairs. This list would include Cornelius Vanderbilt, William K. Vanderbilt, Jay Gould, Leland Stanford, John I. Blair, Collis P. Huntington, G. B. Roberts, F. W. Vanderbilt, Russell Sage, Calvin S. Brice, Charles M. McGhee, Chauncey M. Depew, Chester W. Chapin, John H. Inman, Samuel Sloan, Samuel Thomas, Timothy Hopkins, Frederick L. Ames, James I. Hill, Erastus Corning, Austin Corbin and J. Rogers Maxwell, and the estates of Charles Crocker, Thomas A. Scott, J. W. Garrett, Moses Taylor, Mark Hopkins, Nathaniel Thayer, E. F. Drake, Wm. L. Scott, Wm. Thaw, Horace F. Clark and Sidney Dillon.

Also smaller fortunes have been made by a much larger number of men in a similar way, and by men who were also engaged in banking, mining or other business, and a considerable part of whose wealth was acquired in railway investments. No very definite estimate can be made of the aggregate wealth possessed by these lesser railway millionaires, but we may fairly assume that taking altogether the men who have made large fortunes in railway affairs, their total wealth acquired by this means amounts to at least one-half as much as the present total value of all the railways of the country, about $2,500,000,000 or $3,000,000,000.

But, be this as it may, the indisputable fact remains, that much the largest number of our great millionaires are railway men, and this fact is a significant one for the American people. It shows that the question of cheaper transportation is the greatest economic problem before the American people. It means that a large amount of wealth has been taken from its legitimate channels by men who have been managers of what should be national highways, by exacting extortionate tolls upon the traffic over these highways and thus taxing the industries of the whole country, and is now piled up in these colossal fortunes. It does not stand for legitimate earnings, savings or profits.

For the farmer it has stood for low prices of wheat and cattle and corn, and for high prices of coal and tools and lumber. It stands for mortgages on many farms. For the mechanic, laborer and tradesman it has added to the cost of his food, his tools and his home, and has deprived him of many comforts and luxuries which he should have had, in order to swell the vast fortunes of these railway millionaires.

The average earnings of able-bodied mechanics, farmers and laborers in the United States, those who are fortunate and have work, is less than $500 a year. The average savings of such men who are ordinarily thrifty is less than $100 a year. Mr. Jay Gould has amassed a fortune of about $100,000,000 in the past thirty years by managing and manipulating railway properties. This fortune represents an amount equal to the total earnings of 200,000 busy men for one year ; it represents an amount equal to the total savings of 1,000,000 busy and thrifty men for one year. As the majority of men do not earn or save so much, and as many do not have steady or profitable employment, such a fortune is a greater sum than the total savings of 100,000 ordinary men in a lifetime.

If Ferdinand and Isabella had decreed that Christopher Columbus and his heirs after him should receive a perpetual pension of $250,000 annually from the Spanish government as a reward for his great service in the discovery of a new world, and the amount had been regularly paid from 1492 to this date, the total payments would have amounted to a sum no greater than the present wealth of a Gould, Vanderbilt or Stanford.

As we investigate the problem of our railway management, we shall find that there are many ways in connection with it by which the few are enriched and the many impoverished. As indicated by the proportion of our great millionaires who are railway men, we will find that the present methods of railway management in our country is one of the chief causes for the disparity in the conditions of the people, and one which we have not as yet begun materially to remedy. The railway problem is an important one, and one which urgently demands the attention of the people. The subject is treated at length in several chapters of this work.

John Jacob Astor, William Waldorf Astor and Mrs. William Astor are supposed to be the three wealthiest persons of one family in the world, with possessions valued at about $100,000,000 each. John Jacob Astor, founder of the Astor estate, made a great fortune for his time, by merchandising and in the fur trade, and this fortune, invested in New York real estate in early times, has grown to be the largest estate held in one family, unless it be that of the Vanderbilts.

Commodore Vanderbilt got his start in life in the steamboat business, but he early embarked in railway management and made the bulk of his fortune in that line of business. He was the first of the great railway managers, and was a notable financier. Although the Astor estate had grown to many millions before Vanderbilt was fairly started on the road to wealth, yet the Vanderbilt estate, now owned principally by three sons, amounts to nearly or quite as much as the wealth of the Astors.

The most notable group of millionaires next to the railway managers is composed of the Standard Oil men. Mr. John D. Rockefeller stands with J. J. Astor, William Waldorf Astor, Cornelius Vanderbilt, William K. Vanderbilt, Jay Gould and Leland Stanford, having wealth in the neighborhood of $100,000,000. John D. Rockefeller, Wm. Rockefeller, H. M. Flagler, O. H. Payne, John H. Flagler, Oliver B. Jennings and others, including the estate of Charles Pratt, representing the Standard Oil Trust, have a combined wealth of about $300,000,000.

The best known millionaire next to those already named is Mr. Andrew Carnegie, of Homestead fame. He belongs to a very numerous list of millionaires who have been enabled to build large fortunes by aid of our high protective tariffs. These fortunes have been made in manufactures of iron, steel, glass, cordage, drugs, fabrics; in mining copper, borax, lead, and in many other lines of business which are made very profitable by our tariffs. In many cases protected industries have become monopolies by the practical exclusion of foreign competition, which enabled producers, by combining, to exact exorbitant prices for their products. Pennsylvania furnishes a large list of millionaires of this class.

The *New York Tribune*, in its list of millionaires, publishes the names of 197 in a total of 379 millionaires of Pennsylvania who made their fortunes mainly in protected industries. These fortunes were made mostly in manufactures of iron, steel and glass and in mining coal.

There is a large number of millionaires who have made their wealth mostly in the ownership of pine lands and in the lumber business, which is a protected industry. Michigan has, according to the *Tribune* list, about 50 of this class in a total of 90, more than any other state.

The *Tribune* furnishes a list of names of 1,125 million-aires who made their fortunes mainly in protected indus-tries, in a total list of 4,047. The most striking contrast shown by its summing of classes is as follows:

Number of millionaires who made their fortunes mainly in protected manufacturing, including saw mills and lumber..757.

In unprotected manufacturing................................... 2.

Our government has succeeded by its high tariffs, not only in "nursing infant industries," but in nursing the millionaire industry, as well. This subject is treated at some length in chapters on the tariff.

There is a considerable number of millionaires who have made their fortunes mainly in banking and in merchandizing, but there is no instance of a fortune having been made in either of these lines which amounts to even one-half as much as those of the great railway kings, unless we except the Astor estate, and this was not, for it was built up mainly by the rise in value of New York real estate. Neither bankers, merchants, or men engaged in any other ordinary calling, where there is no special opportunity for controlling an entire line of trade, have furnished any very marked examples of great millionaires. The most prominent of these are A. T. Stew-art, H. B. Claflin, John V. Farwell and Marshall Field among merchants, and F. A. Drexel, A. J. Drexel, J. S. Morgan, J. P. Morgan and the Seligmans among bankers. But neither of these amassed a fortune amounting to but little more than one-fourth as much as those of the great railway magnates, although requiring a longer period of time in acquisition.

The Oil Trust, the Dressed Beef Trust, the Sugar Trust, some protected manufacturing and mining industries and other combinations of capital aside from the railway, telegraph and express lines have often exercised great power in obtaining legislation in their interests. Great wealth in the hands of a few men represents a great and very dangerous power over productive, financial and commercial interests, over legislation and over the conduct of government.

It is this vast power which capitalists and combinations of capitalists have, not only over almost every material interest throughout the land, but over large bodies of mechanics and laborers, over whole communities of men and women in manufacturing and mining districts, that has brought the burning question of the "irrepressible conflict" between capital and labor to a point where it is imperative that the state and national governments shall come in and decide by legislation and by arbitration all differences between such large contending interests. These large fortunes and this vast power in the hands of a few men have been built up, have been made possible, through and by the direct aid of the government and of the whole people ; by franchises, subsidies, bounties, privileges, loans and credits ; by high tariffs and by the protecting hand of a strong government.

That which the government creates it should control. We should not construct engines that we cannot manage when built. We should not help men to build great highways by granting franchises, special privileges and bounties, and when built submit to a direct tax from the men we have aided, by allowing them to "charge what the traffic will bear." If we subsidize favored industries by aid of high protective tariffs which act as a direct tax upon all consumers of the products of such industries, we should at least see that the laborers engaged in them, those who make the wares, should have a fair proportion of the profits. Not only the *industry* but the laborer engaged in it should be protected. It should not be left entirely to capital to say what reward labor shall receive.

Our country should no longer be disgraced and the well-being of the laboring masses jeopardized by strikes and lockouts; by riot, murder and wholesale destruction of property; by the exactions of powerful corporations on the one hand, or the clamors of noisy and unreasonable leaders among employes on the other. It is high time that instead of all this we should have a reign of reason, law and order, and that the questions of rights and compensations between employer and employed shall be decided and enforced by competent authority.

The ultimate solution of this labor question so far as regards the differences between great corporations and their armies of employes will not, however, be found along lines so far suggested. In the case of the transportation problem, the results of legislation and commissions have been found to be only palliative, and the solution of the question is to be found only in the line advocated in the several chapters on that question in *Political Problems.* So in regard to this labor problem, the results of legislation and commissions will be found to be but palliative, and the final solution of the question must come along the same line as will the final remedy for the burdens resulting from our present system of corporate management of the railways.   But, as a present remedy, government arbitration should be resorted to wherever the differences between the conflicting interests cannot be otherwise amicably settled.

We have also the political plutocrats, men who have amassed wealth by managing politics, by getting fat places and holding them for all the money that could be made out of them, by levying tribute upon the people, by jobbery and plunder.   Of such is the political " boss," and some of these have been able to place themselves in the United States Senate.

Most of the men who have made great fortunes in the past thirty years have been enabled to do so by direct aid of the people ; by grants of land ; by credits, subsidies, loans; by franchises and special privileges and immunities : by laws which favored monopolies; and by combinations of capital and power which acted to destroy competition and afford clear fields for the operations of great trusts.   The railways have been, to a large extent, built by subsidies and favors from the people.   The Standard Oil men got special rebates on freight charges from the railways, which alone would have enabled them to kill all competition.   And so by subsidy, special privilege, jobbery and combine are many millionaires made.

It is not a crime to be rich.   A man may be a millionaire and not be a villain   It does not always follow that a man has swindled the people in accumulating a million, but it does follow that he has obtained wealth which he has, as a rule, not earned, and is not justly entitled to. And it follows that the people are not wise in offering premiums to the millionaire industry, in voluntarily paying tribute to it, in furnishing special inducements for its growth. It is among the industries which we do not need to " nurse." It is not on the " infant " list.

It is the man who has but a hundred or a thousand who should be assisted in his endeavors to add to his wealth, rather than the man who has a million or a hundred millions. While we have prated much of " protection to American industry," as the chief and solid corner-stone of our political fabric, we have in fact, in more ways than one, protected the American millionaire industry and failed to protect the industry of the American millions. Perhaps we have undertaken in our day and generation to exemplify literally the words of the Book ; " Unto him who hath much, much shall be given, but unto him who hath little shall be taken away, even that which he hath."

The problem of how to favor the millions, and how not to favor the millionaires, is coming to be an important question with the American people, and will, in the process of time be considered by American statesmen. There are many questions which bear upon this problem and become a part of it, and a large part of this work is devoted to a consideration of some of these questions. We can plainly show how we have been as a people, systematically, blindly going on laboring to enrich the few and impoverish the many, and how we may and should cease to do evil in these ways, and learn to do well by lightening the burdens, smoothing the rugged pathway, and adding to the comfort and the store of the toiling, care-oppressed millions.

A remedy for the perpetuation of millionaire estates by the transmission of wealth from parent to child may be found in a graduated tax upon legacies, making a heavy tax on the estates of millionaires. This subject is treated in the chapters on taxation.

CHAPTER V

INDIVIDUAL HABITS AND CHARACTERISTICS — NATURAL CAUSES AND ENVIRONMENT — THE DRINK HABIT

We find those who are more or less active, industrious, enterprising and frugal and we speak of a combination of these qualities as *thrift*. And we usually find those who are thrifty comfortably provided for even under adverse surroundings, while often the unthrifty are unable to properly care for themselves and families though conditions be favorable.

Thrift and unthrift account for much of the difference in condition between rich and poor. The thrifty are always gathering, always caring for what they have in store : the unthrifty fail to gather as they should, and they allow moth and rust and mice and storm to decimate their supply.

"A penny saved is good as twopence earned." The success of an individual in "getting a start in life " depends upon saving more than upon earning. Wastefulness, extravagance, living close up to or beyond one's income and buying what one cannot pay for : these are guide-posts on the highway to poverty and the almshouse.

To have a provision for a regular income that can be depended upon, is the first requisite to success in life. To be able to do something, and to do that something well — to excel in one's vocation, marks the first mile stone on the highway to a competence or a fortune ; to live within one's income marks the second mile stone ; and the amount which one is able to lay by each month or year " for a rainy day," and the measure of ability to wisely use or invest the savings, determines the relative rapidity with which the mile stones may be passed.

Not that prudence and habits of saving are always virtues, but that they are potent means of acquiring wealth.

Some would-be philosophers tell us that thrift and unthrift account for nearly all of the differences in the material conditions of individuals.   But we know this is not true. We have often seen conditions prevailing where nearly all were well provided for and surrounded by plenty, and we have seen times and places where the many were hard pressed to obtain a comfortable living.

Again we have those who are cunning, grasping and unscrupulous, ready to take any possible advantage of their fellows, ready to take from the widow and the friendless, and to " grind the face of the poor," and for such, as far as may be, the law should prescribe bounds.

NATURAL CAUSES AND ENVIRONMENT

The farmer contends with rocky and barren soils ; with heats and frosts ; with the wet season and the drought ; with weevil, chintz bugs, borers, gophers, rabbits, rats and many other trials and pests.

The merchant is dependent upon the farmer and mechanic. His goods are liable to rust, decay, fade, go out of style, depreciate in value. He often has to pay high rents, insurance, taxes ; sometimes competition is close. There is no business which is not subject to

changes, depressions, annoyances, losses, dull times, and
to the necessity of close, exacting attention in order to
succeed.

All men are more or less creatures of circumstances, of
heredity, of education and early training, of associations
and surroundings, of locality and environment. So that
when we consider the results of experience in any industrial enterprise or under any law or regulation, we should
remember that there are many factors which enter into
almost any problem of human life and human endeavor,
and that it is often difficult to judge the power of any particular cause or force in bringing about the results obtained.

The Drink Habit is one of the most apparent causes of
poverty and distress. It is a thing " known and read of
all men " from the early dawn of history. Wherever the
saloon is, there are found men—the strong, active, and
intelligent as well as the weak and the ignorant—who
should be able to provide abundantly for themselves and
families, but who look " seedy," their wives and children
clothed in shabby garments and their homes becoming
dilapidated. And when it is known of such a man that
" he drinks," that fact sufficiently accounts to the mind
of any one for the man's failure to succeed in the world.

Everyone knows that the man's earnings, which should
have bought food, clothing and other necessaries for the
home, have instead largely gone over the counter of the
saloon. And that while the man's money has gone to the
saloon keeper, that which he received for his money has
been making him day by day less able to obtain work,
and less able to perform his labor. He is not only wasting his substance but wasting his physical energies, and
degrading his manhood.

The drink habit is a most fertile source of poverty, disease and want, and the most prolific cause of demoralization, degradation, pauperism, vice and crime. All this and much more is well known of the evil results of strong drink. The facts are well established and are seldom denied. The vast majority of the people of the United States know something of the magnitude of this evil and concede and appreciate its force and bearing on the moral, physical and financial well being of our people. No man can enumerate all the evils and horrors which follow in its train. Few realize the weight of this burden upon our people.

CHAPTER VI

COST OF THE DRINK TRAFFIC

The people of the United States pay about *one thousand million dollars a year* for liquors. Statistics are often unreliable. In many cases it is impossible to get reliable data for showing cost or waste, or loss or gain, in important matters in regard to which we need the facts. In many things we can make only estimates.

As to the amount of the nation's drink bill, we have exact data from which to make up the bulk of the account. It is a plain business proposition. The production of liquor is directly under national supervision, and the

Internal Revenue Department shows the amount of liquors " withdrawn for consumption " each year. For 1889 there was of :

Domestic distilled spirits - - 70,000,000 gals.
"   "   wines   -   30,000,000 "
"   fermented liquors   -   25,000,000 bbls.

Any one by learning the retail prices for liquors can readily compute the approximate cost of these amounts to the people. By adding one-fifth to the quantity of distilled " proof spirits " for reduction to the strength as ordinarily retailed, and counting it at six dollars per gallon as an average price as sold by the glass, counting the wine at two dollars per gallon, and beer at eighteen dollars per barrel (at five cents per half pint glass it would amount to twenty-four dollars per barrel) we have the cost at retail as follows :

Domestic distilled spirits -   - $500,000,000
"   wines   -   60,000,000
"   fermented liquors   -   450,000,000
Imported   "   20,000,000
Illicit, smuggled and home made }
liquors, estimated   -   } 20,000,000
                                 _____
                                 $1,050,000,000

Mr. F. N. Barrett, editor of the *American Grocer*, at the request of the Chief of the Bureau of Statistics, submitted a report on this subject, based on the Government statistics for the year 1886, in which he made the direct retail cost for liquors for that year to be $700,000,000. His figures must be conservative for he thought the " fanatical advocates " had made their sum too large. Mr. Edward Atkinson, about the same time made a computation agreeing with that of Mr. Barrett. The amount of liquors

consumed in 1889 was greater than in 1886. Some estimate the nation's liquor bill to be $1,100,000,000 a yeai,
and we may consider one billion as a fair calculation.

This sum represents the first cost of the liquor to the
people who drink, and is a total loss to the consumers.
It is a sum which should be paid for food and clothing,
for houses and lands, for tools and furniture, for books
and periodicals, for churches and schools, for carrying on
the business of life. It is an immense sum. It represents
a fearful waste. But it is only a part of the cost of the
drink traffic to the drinkers and to the nation. The
liquors are not only of no possible benefit to those who
use them, but are a positive injury. They do not give
health or strength or vigor. They do not make the brain
clearer or the step more elastic. They cause weakness and
sickness, disorders of the body and the mind. So far as
the drinkers are concerned, this vast sum would be far
better cast into the sea, than to be spent for that which de-
stroys character and manhood, wastes fortunes and blasts
lives. No man can enumerate all the evils which follow in
the train of the drink traffic, but we can tell enough.
We must add to the cost of the liquors in order to approximate the total cost of the drink traffic, other items as follows:

1. Lost Labor. From loss of health and strength and
endurance, from loss of character, from loss of time and
opportunity, from loss of place. Loss from debauch and
sickness and imprisonment. Loss from enfeebled mind and
shortened lives. Some rate the loss of productive ability
from drink to be equal to the cost of the drink—that the
ordinary drinker, especially the hard drinker, as a rule, loses
in this way in a lifetime, as much as the drink costs. Probably a fair estimate is to place it at one-third as much.

2. Cost of Sickness from Drink. Expense of care, board and medical service. Some careful computations go to show that there are on an average about one hundred and fifty thousand persons sick at all times from the use of liquors, and that it costs fifty thousand dollars a year to care for them.

3. Cost of Crime from Drink. At least three-fourths of the crimes are caused by the use of liquors. A large part of the cost of police service, of criminal courts and officials and of prisons and reformatories is made necessary by drink. The cost of arrests, trials and imprisonment, from being "drunk and disorderly," and from graver crimes caused by intemperance, becomes a large tax upon the people, estimated at $35,000,000 a year.

4. Cost of Pauperism and Insanity Caused by Drink. Estimated at $15,000,000.

The figures here given show the annual cost of the liquor traffic in the United States to be :

Cost of liquors - - -	$1,000,000,000
Loss of labor - - - -	330,000,000
Loss from sickness - - - -	50,000,000
" " crime - - -	35,000,000
" pauperism and insanity -	15,000,000
Total,	$1,430,000,000

As an offset to this we have municipal, state and national taxes paid by the liquor traffic, about $135,000,000 per year. And we suppose the traffic should receive credit for the amounts paid for fruits, grains and other material, and for labor used in manufacture of liquors. But after making all reasonable reductions we would still have as the cost and loss to the nation each year for drink, over one billion dollars in cash.

Data for making these computations has been taken from "The Encyclopedia of Temperance and Prohibition," by Funk and Wagnalls.

But we have so far been enumerating only the direct cost and loss to the people who use the liquors and the amounts needed for their care, correction and maintenance. Besides, there is the sickness, wounds, insanity and death in the families of the drinkers caused by want, exposure, neglect and cruel treatment,and also the attendant poverty which makes the drinker's family often a burden upon society.

And is this all ? Shall we take no account of the sorrow, the suffering, the shame, the disgrace? Can we measure the deep degradation and misery of the drunkard or the untold anguish and the bitter desolation of the drunkard's wife and children ? Can we conceive of the heartache, the dread, the despair of the drunkard's father and mother? Shall we consider only food, raiment and shelter for the body, and have no thought for the peace and comfort and happiness of the mind ? Are truth, and honor, and virtue and sobriety not to be weighed in the balance? And shall we take no account of the tens of thousands of human lives destroyed each year by this drink plague?

CHAPTER VII

SPECULATION IN LAND—THE CREDIT SYSTEM

More notable, more sweeping, more wholly wasteful and disastrous to communities than almost any other cause of poverty and loss, is speculation in land. Like measles and scarlet fever, it appears, now here, now there. It comes on gradually and increases in force and volume. It is infectious. Men and women take it from their friends, and inhale it from the air. It regards neither age, sex, color or " previous condition of servitude."

Banker and barber, preacher and doctor, farmer and merchant, servant girl and washerwoman, yes, the widow and the orphan, all alike bring their tribute, they bring often all they have—houses, lands, homes—and cast it on the flood-tide of speculation and see it swept out into the remorseless sea of utter waste and loss.

Like the appetite for drink, or passion for the game, it grows on one. It is insidious, seductive, enticing ; and apparently legitimate, respectable and safe.

Some men can drink or can let it alone ; the ordinary man can not. Some can win large stakes and quit with a full purse, but that is not the usual way.

For a time, speculation in land is a winning venture, and the greater the gains and the longer continued, the more wholly is the speculator absorbed in the game. But by and by the end approacheth, and the man who " can drink or can let it alone " quits, while the multitude go on to financial ruin.

The man who begins to speculate in land, like a man who puts "a mortgage on the farm," is starting on the road to penury and want. Every "boom" in land values is bound to come to an untimely end, and the higher the fever and the greater the boom, the greater the disaster when the end comes.

Somewhere we read of "land hunger," with the Oklahoma boom as an example showing how "hungry" men are for land. In Los Angeles, during its third and latest boom, men stood in line all night, or hired substitutes to hold their places, in order to be among the first in the morning to have a chance to select lots in a proposed town out on a rocky, barren waste. Probably some of these same Los Angeles boomers were "in at the death" at Oklahoma.

Away in Winnepeg, Manitoba, men bought town lots which they never saw, at auction by lamplight. This kind of "land hunger" is not of the kind which tends to make two blades of grass to grow where only one grew before. Indianapolis, Kansas City, Fort Smith, Wichita, Denver, San Diego, Los Angeles, Seattle and Tacoma and most of the towns and cities of the country have had their booms and their depressions.

And this is not only the case with town property, but farm lands also have their periods of exalted and fictitious values and of depressions below the point of intrinsic worth. Many a farmer has lost a good farm by trying to possess one or two more. To be "land poor" is to be poor indeed.

Buying something which one does not need because it seems cheap, with the hope of selling to some one who does need it at a higher price, is always a risky undertaking. Things so bought are often found to be very dear before they are sold. Every period and phase of undue exaltation is bound to be followed by its period of undue depression.

An elderly gentleman who passed through the Indianapolis boom, says that after the boom had collapsed he paid out sixty thousand dollars in good money to try to save his property and then lost it all. That "Truth is stranger than fiction" is exemplified in the history of any great real estate boom.

In the unwritten history of the great boom in Southern California in 1886 and 1887 one might find abundant material for the wildest romance, and that by telling a "plain unvarnished tale."

Thousands of good people, all sorts of people, almost whole communities, those who were ordinarily careful, saving, penurious, as well as the extravagant and venturesome, launched out on the sea of speculation and suddenly became wealthy. They counted not their wealth by hundreds or by thousands, but by tens of thousands, hundreds of thousands and millions.

And then, in a few months, the boom rolled by and most of these people found themselves poor. The most of them so poor that they could not pay their debts, and they had a hard time of it to "keep body and soul together." They didn't have roast beef and turkey so often, but were glad to get mush and potatoes.

Men who in 1887 had bank transactions footing up many thousands each month, in 1889 did not know how to make a turn to pay for another sack of flour.

While the great and long extended boom of Kansas City was drawing its last breath, and the high flown boom of Southern California was suffering from a bad state of collapse, Denver was at the zenith of its exaltation, and the lively boom at Seattle and Spokane was in the acme of its glory. Now, at the close of 1891, while Southern California has succeeded fairly well in pulling itself together after its great disaster, Denver real estate is hunting lower levels, and the glory of Spokane, Seattle and Tacoma and the "Sound Country" is waning from its highly exalted state.

Besides, when men think they are making money rapidly they are almost sure to spend rapidly, and to become extravagant and wasteful. It is not at all a difficult matter to spend money. "Easy come easy go." And so it follows that, while the speculation goes on lively, a large per cent of the amount handled is expended, consumed or wasted in one way and another ; in buildings, equipages, furniture, servants, travels, amusements, fine clothes, dissipations and the thousand ways known to man and to woman. In this way the accumulations made by years of hard earning and careful saving are in a short time swept into nothingness. What was not lost by the venture is lost by fast living. By the bunghole or the spigot it all goes. Wealth so spent is swept out of existence as much as if by fire or flood. Though it be "an ill wind that blows nobody good," yet what is lost to the individual is, in the main, lost to the state.

During the speculative period production is reduced to zero, because all the producers have become speculators, and consumption has been raised to a hundred (or a thousand) because all the speculators are "millionaires of a day."

It follows as the outcome of the speculation, that the community as a whole is a great loser ; that the vast majority of the people have suffered a very serious loss, and that for many individuals, the loss is well-nigh irretrievable. Some localities and some individuals are gainers, but only to a small extent of the total loss. As a whole it counts heavily on the debtor side.

Speculation, and especially speculation in land, is one of the great causes of poverty, loss and disaster to the individual and to the state, and calls for remedies wherever and whenever practicable. Not "land monopoly," but "land speculation" is the greater evil so far as the land question is concerned.

The great financial panics and disasters of our own and other countries have been caused largely by speculation. The panics of 1837, 1857 and 1873, in the judgment of our most careful historians, were mainly the result of speculation.

THE CREDIT SYSTEM

As the social evil depends largely for its life and growth, on its twin vice, drink, so does the evil of speculation in land depend to a great extent for its vitality and magnitude, on its twin evil, the credit system. Did men buy only what they paid for, the risk of loss in speculation would not be nearly so great.

It is true that men often begin to speculate in a careful, moderate way, just as the man who takes his first glass begins in a moderate way. But the temptation to "invest" induces him first to buy something which in order to pay for requires capital which he needs in his business or for his living, and then the prospect of large gains tempts him to buy on a partial payment, hoping to sell and realize a profit before further payments fall due.

And so it comes about that the amateur speculator who began with a good resolution of " pay as you go," and with a righteous fear of a mortgage, more and more gets to buying as much as possible with the capital in hand by buying where the least payment can be made. In speculation, the greater the hazard, the greater the gain, and the greater the loss in the end if one waits to the end (as most do) for a " round up." The men who "can drink or can let it alone," (and you know how many there are who can do that!) could perhaps be trusted to speculate in land by buying on partial payments, but those who can not be sure of control over their appetites should not begin.

But, aside from buying land or other things on speculation without paying for them, in buying anything which one does not pay for there is risk and danger. Remember that unpaid bills at the stores and shops are very apt to bring a mortgage on the farm. And the bills and the mortgage, either or both, are very likely to take the farm sooner or later.

You may be poor, be " hard run," have to wear a patched coat and live on bread and potatoes, but, once get a home and have it paid for, and buy only what you pay for, and you will always have a place of your own while you live, and the widow and the children will have a place to call home if you leave them behind when you go to your final home.

There are occasions when it is proper and expedient for individuals, or cities or states to incur debt, but a debt is a burden as a rule wherever it is, and should be avoided and lightened and lifted whenever possible. Every man starting out in business, or undertaking to retrieve his fallen fortune and get on a solid footing, should make it a cardinal principle of business to " Pay as you go." If you can't pay, don't go.

CHAPTER VIII

MONOPOLIES AND TRUSTS

Among the most apparent causes of poverty are the great giants which have arisen in these latter days; those creatures of the Plutocrats which have bodies, heads, arms and "sacks," but no souls ; which are often possessed with great vigor and vitality, and which never tire, never get sick, never grow old and never die ; which are able to wear out, tire out and crush out of existence all small competitors, and in whose grasp the laboring man is but as the hare in the clutch of the wolf. Those stern rulers which exact tribute from the people, whatever they do or whichever way they go, and tax them upon almost everything which they produce or consume. These are the autocrats who rule us with a relentless sway, who domineer us and scourge us and hedge us about and drive us to the wall.

The octopus, or devil-fish, is a denizen of the deep most dreaded by man. Whatever comes within its reach is clutched by its long arms, drawn into its embrace, and beneath the deep waters its life is crushed out. The

monopoly is the octopus of the business world.   It reaches
out its powerful arms and crushes the life out of any
competing business.   Where monopoly comes competition
must go.

And what do our great political leaders—those sentinels
of ours who stand upon the outer wall that they may be
ready to cry aloud when danger approaches—tell us about
the trusts ?   Do they see danger?   And do they tell us
how to avert it, or defend ourselves from its attacks?
Hear what they say : James G. Blaine, the great Captain,
says :

" Well, I shall not discuss trusts this afternoon.   I shall
not venture to say that they are advantageous or dis-
advantageous.   They are largely private affairs, with
which neither President Cleveland nor any private citizen
has any particular right to interfere."

So, you see, these trusts are not such dangerous things
after all.   Mr. Blaine is a brilliant leader and ought to
know about them.   Perhaps we have been imposed upon
by the talk about monopolies.

Mr. Thomas B. Reed, the republican leader in Congress,
speaks of "the great new Chimera Trusts," and says :
" *Outside the patent office there are no monopolies in this
country, and there never can be.   A dozen men fix the prices
for sixty million freemen !   They can never do it.*"

Mr. Andrew Carnegie also denies the existence of monopolies in this country.   He says they are impossible.

Mr. McKinley says he has no sympathy with combinations organized to control the supply and thereby
control prices, and he speaks of "the oil trust and the
whiskey trust which are so commanding and powerful,
which make prices and alter them."   He claims, however,
that there is nothing in our tariff laws to promote or even

suggest monopolies. He then goes on to say : "There is a trust or combination made up of all the plate-glass manufacturers of Europe."

Now, if all the plate-glass manufacturers of Europe can combine and control prices, why not all the plate-glass manufacturers of America? And if all the plate-glass manufacturers can combine, why not all the manufacturers of window glass, and steel rails, and steel beams, and white lead, and cordage, and jute bags, and copper, and borax, and a lot of other things ? Most assuredly they can and do. These combinations are on every hand and in almost every line of business.

This is an era of trusts. During the last two decades there has been a great increase in the number and power of business combinations. We have seen one kind of business after another go under the control of a combine. It would be difficult to enumerate all the many branches of business now controlled mainly by a combination. We have monopolies in the trade in beef, borax, bags, coal, copper, coffins, lumber, land, lead, sugar, salt, telegraphs, telephones, twine and in many other lines of business.

The monopolies in transportation and communication are the greatest and most oppressive, and the question of the ownership and management of the railway and tele-graph lines is the greatest economic question now coming before the American people. These questions will be found treated at length in Part III.

CHAPTER IX

UNWISE TAXATION

A considerable part of the burdens of the industrial classes in this country is chargeable to our unwise methods of taxation. Probably in no other enlightened nation is there to be found a system of taxation so unwise, so vicious as our own—so oppressive to the poor, so partial to the rich. From taxes upon imposts to taxes upon " beds, bedding and cooking things," do we carry out our unstatesmanlike methods of putting the greater proportion of burdens upon those who are least able to bear them, and of favoring those who have the greatest ability to pay the cost of government maintenance. This is true in a larger degree in some states than in others.

California presents the extreme of our cumbersome and burdensome methods of taxation. In this state, a poor widow whose sole earthly possessions consist of a small stock of poor household goods, a slender wardrobe, a cow and some chickens, and who is unable by dint of the most persistent toil and the exercise of the most pinching economy to decently support herself and her children, is compelled by the law of the state to pay the usual rate of tax upon her pittance of property. Such a tax is an outrage upon common decency. It is barbarous. Those who are unable to bear burdens should not be compelled to bear them. In exacting taxes from the very poor, we but emulate the example of those despots who compel their poorest serfs to pay to the ruler a proportion of all they produce.

We also tax mortgages with the intent of making the holder of the mortgage pay a part of the tax on the property, but the man who loans money always exacts an additional per cent to cover the mortgage tax.

In some states a limited amount of property is exempted from taxation, and in this way the poor are favored. In but very few instances do we lay a tax upon incomes. The income is the best measure of ability to pay taxes.

As the subject of taxes upon imports is made the chief issue between the old political parties, the tariff question is treated as a whole in the next two chapters. Other questions relating to taxation are treated in Part III.

CHAPTER X

THE TARIFF—TRUST TARIFF—CLOG TARIFF

A tariff is a tax laid on imports or exports. A *protective tariff* is a tax on imports of articles produced, or which it is thought should be produced, in the country. A *non-protective tariff* is a tax on imports of articles not produced in the country, that is, not profitably produced or in any sufficient quantity for the needs of the country. *Free trade* is the absence of tariff. The term "free trade tariff" is a misnomer, and the term free trade is loosely used in tariff discussions, and is misleading.

The policy of our government has been mainly protective. We tax a long list of articles which we produce to a greater or less extent, and we admit many articles free of duty, but we do not, as a rule, have non-protective (or " revenue ") tariffs. All nations have tariffs. Most nations have tariffs similar to ours. Some nations have export duties, but we do not. Great Britain and Holland have no protective tariffs. They have non-protective tariffs and free trade. France, Germany, Italy and most nations have protective tariffs.

The primary and legitimate objects of a protective tariff are to "nurse infant industries " by placing such tax upon the foreign article as will shield the producer until he can secure such necessary capital, machinery, skilled labor and experience, as will enable him to successfully compete with his foreign rival, and to continue the tax while such protection is needed. The rate of tax being justly apportioned so as to encourage and foster economic and profitable production but not exorbitant prices. It should not be prohibitory.

The argument for protection is, that a nation should, as far as practicable, produce all the things it needs or can make profitable for export, thus diversifying its industries and employing its capital and labor, instead of paying tribute to foreign capital and foreign labor, and also thus adding to the market for its home products.

In many cases, beyond question, important American industries have been established and built up by the aid of a protective tariff, and in many cases, beyond question, burdensome monopolies have been fostered and upheld by the same means.

In what cases, and to what extent such protection should be given is a question to be decided in each case by a careful consideration of the needs, the importance and the merits of each industry.

The argument for a non-protective (or "revenue") tariff, is that it is a tax, pure and simple, borne equally by all the consumers and paid directly to the government, while a protective tariff is a tax paid alike by all the consumers, but which goes partly or wholly, as the case may be, to the producer—that a protective tariff is a tax upon the people of one class or locality to benefit those of another, and as such is primarily unjustifiable, and leads to wide partiality and discrimination.

The argument for *free trade* is that there should be no restrictions upon legitate industry or trade ; that the citizen should be allowed to produce that which he can produce most profitably, and to buy where he can buy cheapest and sell where he can sell dearest ; that nations should produce the things which they can produce cheaper than other nations, and buy of other nations the things which they can not as profitably produce at home.

A tariff, at least a high tariff, on articles which we produce as cheaply as other nations, brings little revenue, and as a rule, does not benefit the nation, but tends to foster monopoly, and is not properly a protective, but a *trust tariff*. The trust tariff is not always a tax upon the consumer. Sometimes it is and sometimes it is not, but its tendency is that way and it acts as a premium upon monopoly. When, by its aid, the producer is enabled to pay freights and then sell his goods cheaper in the foreign market than he sells at home, the trust tariff accomplishes its mission.

By it the manufacturer or producer is enabled to exact a price for his product above reasonable cost and profit of production, and this charge becomes a direct tax upon the consumer to enrich the producer, *and the government has used its strong arm to compel the many to pay tribute to the few.*

A legitimate protective tariff is a beneficent measure, but a trust tariff becomes a curse to any people. A tariff that is practically prohibitory in any article which admits of a combination of producers, tends to establish and maintain trusts.

We also have under the guise of protection what should be termed *clog tariffs*, which may be in a measure protective, but which to a larger extent are a clog upon industry. These are tariffs on raw or partly manufactured materials needed by our manufacturers and not produced by us in sufficient quantity, and which, if our manufacturers could obtain as cheaply as their foreign rivals, would enable them to supply our home market with the finished product and often to make their goods a profitable export.

While it remains the duty of the nation, as of the individual, to provide first for its own, the protective policy should be adopted and retained in cases where it best subserves the interests of all its people, and in cases where protection of any particular industry does not " promote the general welfare " we should have free trade.

The old, old question of whether protection or non-protection should be the policy of our government should not monopolize the time and thought of our national law makers so far to the exclusion of questions of vastly greater importance to the American people. We should not deal with *theories*, but with *conditions*—not fancies, but facts.

One industry needs protection, another does not. One is a grinding monopoly, another struggles for bare existence. To apply the theory of protection to any industry regardless of its needs, its importance and its merits is unwise. To apply the theory of free trade to all is equally unwise. But let no citizen be alarmed. The country needs no great or sudden change of the tariff, and *in any event there will be none.* No party and no considerable proportion of the people contemplate such a change. The Mills Bill, with a large surplus in the treasury, proposed a reduction of about seven per cent, from forty-seven to forty per cent. The McKinley Bill with a decreasing surplus made a raise of about the same per cent. (In many cases too high, no doubt.)

The ignorant, the partisan, the stalwart, the blind and deaf advocates of protection claim that it *always* benefits and is never an injury to a nation—that it *never* fosters wasteful production, exorbitant prices, or monopoly. Similar advocates of free trade or of revenue tariffs claim that protection is *always* an injury and never a benefit. Between these two extremes there must be, there always has been and always will be, a mean of reason and of common sense.

When any industry has been "protected" for a long term of years ; when it has at command ample capital, machinery, skill and experience ; when it no longer needs a nurse ; then if it can not compete with the foreign rival while having the advantage of saving the cost of transportation and importers' profit, the question of continuing its protection should be well considered before asking the people to longer pay tribute to it. In some cases it is better to still give it the benefit of a moderate tariff, and in others to let it stand on its own bottom.

It is a question of compensations ; whether, if an industry can not succeed without protection, the advantage to be gained from the capital and labor kept at home and from the added market thus given to other products, offsets the cost to the people. In the end it is a question of "the survival of the fittest" and the best.

The question of customs duties is a *business* question, and should be considered from a clear, unbiased, business stand-point ; and not from a partisan, a sectional or a selfish one.

A permanent tariff commission, composed of business men who thoroughly understand the needs of production and of trade, and who are broad enough to consider each question on its merits and on the principle of promoting the general welfare of all the people, would be the kind of body to decide these questions for us.

The tariff *is not a question to be settled*, except as to the manner of treating it. The tariff like "The poor ye have always with you." We shall always be, at least we should always be, "revising the tariff." *How to revise the tariff?* Whether this or that article shall be taxed ? If taxed whether 10, 20, 40 or 80 per cent ? Whether this or that article shall be added to or taken from the free list ? These questions we will always be obliged to consider.

Let the American people see the tariff question in its true light, giving it the importance it demands, no more, then there will be no difficulty in properly treating it. But, before that time will come it must be divested of party spirit, of sectional jealousy, of blind prejudice and of selfish interest.

An objection to all taxes on imports is that they are taxes on what we use and consume; on food, clothing, tools, etc; largely on the most common necessaries of life, and paid in almost equal proportion by the poor and rich

alike. A law which compels the weak to bear as much
burden as the strong, and the poor to pay as much tax
as the rich, is not a just measure unless it has advantages
for all the people which more than offset this defect.

CHAPTER XI

THE TARIFF QUESTION AS A SUPREME ISSUE

The question of the tariff, protective or non-protective,
high or low, is *not* a question of paramount importance
to the American people. It really merits but a small
share of time or space. But for the false position it has
been made to occupy by the old parties, it would very
soon lose place as an issue.

As questions pertaining to the war could no longer be
made to serve, no other question seemed available as the
leading issue for the campaign of 1884 but that of tariff.
And so it was brought out, aired and brushed, had some
new clothes made, was treated by electricity and heavily
stimulated until it had enough vitality infused into it to
enable it to stand and defy competition.

And it is now the prime mission of the old time serving parties to stand as its backers and see that it holds
the boards against all comers as long as possible. While
they succeed in this, their " calling and election is sure."
What else can they do ? They seek no new questions:
they champion no reforms : they want no farther division
of voters : they deprecate new issues : they are content
with present conditions.

As a chief issue, the tariff question has been highly exalted ; each side trying to make black appear white, or white appear black as the case might be. The one claiming that what we need is a high, practically prohibitive tariff, and that that is "protection to American Industry ;" the other that we should have a tariff for revenue with protection as a mere incident. The nation needs neither the one nor the other. It *does* need such protection as shields industries which need protection, and yields needed revenue, but does not tend to encourage monopolies or trusts, to unduly enrich the manufacturer at the expense of the consumer, or unduly protect the producer at a greater cost to the manufacturer or the nation. *And this is what we would have if the question were non-partisan.*

And so we have two sets of advocates, who, lawyer-like, strive to make the worse appear the better reason, and, as far as possible, to distract the jury. The tariff "has the floor." There is no possible prospect for any other cause while it absorbs attention. So it is not a matter of choice. We *must* attack it. We must wrestle with it. We must overcome it and hurl it from its unmerited position before we can secure any hearing for other questions which press for solution. We must take it up and examine its fabric to learn of what material it is composed. Most of the tariff discussion is made up of certain statements, comparisons and conclusions in regard to things which have little bearing upon the subject and yet become the stock arguments and are made to do duty on all occasions. I will give the principal ones.

1. Wages are much higher in the United States, which has .	2. Wages are much higher in England, which has free trade,

protection, than in England, which has free trade, consequently protection makes high wages and free trade makes low wages.

3. Wages are much higher in the United States now under a high tariff than they were forty years ago under a low tariff. Consequently high tariff causes high wages and low tariff causes low wages.

5. The "free trade toilers" of England emigrate to the United States in order to get better wages and a chance to improve their condition, which shows conclusively that free trade depresses and degrades a people while protection lifts them to a higher plane of civilization.

7. Manufactured articles are much cheaper in the United States now under a high tariff than they were forty years ago under a low tariff, which shows that a high tariff gives us cheap goods and a low tariff makes things dear.

than in Germany and France which have protection, therefore free trade makes high wages and protection makes low wages.

4. Wages are much higher in England now under free trade than they were fifty years ago under protection, therefore free trade causes high wages and protection causes low wages.

6. The poor, unpaid, "protected" mill hands of Germany and France emigrate to free trade England in order to get better wages and to find the better conditions where trade is unrestricted, which shows beyond a doubt that "protection," so called, hampers and grinds a people while free trade improves their condition.

8. Goods are much cheaper in England now with free trade than they were under protection. Thus we see that protection made high priced goods and free trade gave them cheaper products.

The advocates of protection or non-protection, as the case may be, in using either of the cases here cited as an argument, assume that the kind and rate of tariff in a country determines the rate of wages, the prices of goods, the condition of the laborer, and the general welfare of the people. He is oblivious to all differences of area, of time, of climate, of agricultural and mineral wealth, of inventions and machinery, of ability and thrift of the people, and of the many conditions which affect the productive power and material prosperity of a nation.

Wages are much higher in Germany than in Italy, higher in France than in Germany, and still much higher in free trade England than in those and all other countries of Europe which have protection. And wages are still higher in the United States than in England. And these facts sufficiently show that the tariff of a country does not determine its rate of wages, the prices of its goods, or the condition of its people. It is but one of many factors.

Besides, the wage is one thing and what a man can buy with his wages is another. A wage of two dollars a day may be no more in purchasing power in one country or period, than one dollar and a half or even one dollar in another.

And remember that *labor is not protected.* The manufacturer may be, but he employs those who will do his work for the least money. They come to us from Germany, from Italy, from Canada, from the corners of the earth. There are no bars—no gates. *In labor there is free trade.*

Economists talk of the "iron law of wages." It means nothing. There is no law of prices in anything where there is free trade, except the law of supply and demand. Men buy where they can buy cheapest and sell where they can sell dearest. The employer considers not whether his hireling dines on bread and meat or on mush and potatoes ; whether he wears denims or tweeds ; whether he dwells in a house or a hovel ; but, how cheaply can he hire him. You say the employer is human and considers the comfort of his men. Yes, sometimes. Usually the employer is a corporation, which has a body and a head but no soul.

Advocates of high and of low tariff also cite us to different periods in our history, claiming that the conditions either of prosperity or adversity were owing to the kind of tariff in force for the period. The principal historical facts used as arguments are given below :

9. Following the protective tariffs of 1824–28 came the "Compromise tariff" of 1833, which provided for a reduction of ten per cent every two years. This reduction produced a depression which finally culminated in the great financial disaster of 1837, thus showing to the people the dire effects of a low tariff.

10. The reduction of the tariff in 1833 gave a decided impetus to all kinds of business throughout the States. The panic of 1837 was caused by wild cat money and wild speculation, begun in a time of great prosperity. Mr. Blaine, the great advocate of protection said: "The years 1834, 1835 and 1836 were distinguished by all manner of business hazard, there was a great stimulus to manufacturing and to trade, which finally assumed the form of dangerous speculation." Henry Clay said it was speculation in land and the expansion of the currency that produced the panic of 1837, and that the reduction of the tariff had nothing to do with it.

11. The "free trade tariff" of 1846, during a period of eleven years led up to and produced its usual results, by bringing on the great financial panic of 1857.

12. The reduction of the tariff in 1846 was followed by ten years of unexampled prosperity, so much so that the people again went wild with speculation and this caused the great panic of 1857.

13. It is true that the tariff of 1846 was followed by ten years of prosperity, but this was not caused by the low tariff but by various "adventitious circumstances," namely, the war with Mexico, the Irish famine, the discovery of gold in California, and the Crimean war; but when these had passed and the people were left with their ordinary resources, then the disaster came.

14. In 1846 the representatives in Congress from New England, at that time the principal manufacturing district of the country, almost unanimously opposed the reduction of the tariff. But after this reduction had been in operation eleven years, the same representation voted almost unanimously for a further reduction from an average of twenty-eight per cent to an average of twenty-one per cent, which shows that they thought the reduction had been a benefit and not an injury to the country.

15. For the last thirty years the United States has had protection while England has had free trade. During that period of time our advancement in material growth, population and wealth has been remarkable, greatly exceeding that of free trade England, which furnishes undeniable proof that our prosperity has been the legitimate outgrowth of our protective system.

16. England with free trade has increased more rapidly in population and wealth in the last thirty years than have France, Germany and Italy under protection, which shows conclusively that her prosperity has been caused by free trade. If our prosperity for thirty years has been caused by protection, what caused the great financial and business depression from 1873 to 1879 (the panic of '77,) and what has caused the great increase in farm mortgages, and in the proportion of tenant farmers, and the decrease in the value of farm lands?

Any one of these arguments (?) is sufficient upon which to base a broad and eloquent address, and be a final answer to all grounds of controversy ! It is a palpable instance of blind obliviousness to all the facts in the case but one, and that the one the lawyer magnifies. Especially do the advocates of protection delight to enlarge and amplify upon the boundless resources and the marvelous growth, prosperity and wealth of the great American nation, and to claim it as the result of our protective system. As put by Mr. Blaine : " Can Mr. Gladstone show a parallel ? " Any good " Fourth-of-July " speech would serve for an argument in this line.

As a fine sample of resounding and effulgent eloquence in the halls of Congress on this theme, I give the following from the great protection leader, Mr. Thomas B. Reed, in his speech on the Mills bill.

" Whoever takes down the map of 1860 and the map of 1888 will look upon the most wondrous growth that ever the sun shone on in all its myriad courses around the earth. It is a marvelous spectacle. It is not alone the great cities, born like exhalations, which flash prosperity over the great lakes, over the broad plains, over the mighty fields rich with verdure or teeming with uncounted harvests. It is the fact that all this wealth and prosperity has been so shaped that it seeks the comfort not of the rich, not of the lounging owner of fixed income, not of the pampered minion of governmental power, but of the plain people whom Abraham Lincoln loved, and who are of right the chief glory of this Republic."

And this is all owing to our " protection to American industry." That term has a wonderfully attractive, taking, assuring ring. It shows that protection is the *sine qua non*. It seems to take the honest son of toil by the hand and lift him clear out of his slough of despond. It shows him that protection seeks first *his* uplift and betterment. It redounds not to the profit of the rich.

("Protection has proved a distributer of great sums of money, not an agency for amassing it in the hands of the few." Blaine.)

Millions of sturdy toilers have been induced by that assuring song of "protection to American industry" to give a vote to help the "protected" millionaire owners of copper mines, and borax trusts, and white lead combines, and pine forests, and glass works, and steel rail mills to add another million to their limited store so that the families of these poor millionaires should not come to want!

We need not question whether or no our tariff has been a chief cause of our prosperity. We need not search for causes for our prosperity. We see them on every hand. Rather should we ask, why the adversity? and is the tariff one of the causes of our adversity?

With our diverse, our immense, our limitless natural resources of valleys and plains, forests and mines ; our active and enterprising people ; our wonderful inventions; our multiplied machines by which one man does the work of three, or of ten, or of thirty, and with steam and electricity harnessed to the wheels ; with our ability to produce vastly beyond the capacity of any other people on the globe ; the question which should stare us in the face, which should press, and grind and burn for solution is, " Why, with all these resources do we fail to provide for so many of our people ? " Why does the New York sewing woman, to save body and soul from perdition, have to " wear her fingers to the quick" for seventy cents a day? Why the thousands who would work, but find none ? Why the hunger and want ? Why do farms go under the hammer by the thousands ? Why ?

The politician cries peace, peace, when there is no peace ;
he tells how great, how prosperous, how happy we are !
Great is the Trust, prosperous the Plutocrat, and happy
he who gathereth the farms with his mortgage "as a hen
gathereth her chickens under her wings ! "

Among the things about this vexed tariff question
which it is difficult for a lay-man to understand, is, why,
if the country was highly prospered from 1846 to 1857
under an average tariff of twenty-eight per cent, we now
need tariffs as high as shown in the following list ?

Window glass	-	-	123 to 138 per cent
Pocket knives	-	-	-	75 "
Knit underwear	-	-	112 to 147 "
Blankets, flannels and hats,	110 "
Ready-made clothing	-	-	84 "
Dress goods	-	-	-	73 to 110 "
Woolen yarns	-	-	-	100 "

It seems to be a sound proposition, that any industry
which needs a tariff of one hundred per cent to sustain it,
is not worth sustaining. It does not pay us to manufacture
an article which costs us two dollars to produce, when we
can buy such an article of foreign make equally as good
for one dollar. That means that the farmer must pay
two bushels of wheat for an article worth but one bushel,
in order to "protect American industry."

Reciprocity, or mutual protection with other countries,
is a wise device of the protectionist. By pushing this
measure to the front, Mr. Blaine, in 1888, scored a victory
for the republican party, while his stalwart, high tariff
compeers were doing their "level best" to "pluck defeat
from the jaws of victory" by talking of high tariff.

Among the most common fallacies used as an argument

by the advocates of free trade (and of which Mr. Roger Q. Mills is a most able advocate and as stalwart on that extreme as Mr. Thomas B. Reed is on the other,) is that the prosperity of a nation is shown by the extent of its foreign commerce, and that the more we *buy* of foreign nations the more we are able to *sell* to them. As well say that the prosperity of the farmer is shown by the amount of his trade at the stores—that the more he *buys* of the merchant the more he will be able to *sell* to him.

The prosperity of the nation and of the individual depends upon skill, ability and enterprise in production and sale, and upon economy in consumption and purchase. To supply as far as possible the home needs by home production, to produce as much as possible for sale, and to buy as little as may be for home consumption, is the true, plain and *only* way for the individual or the nation to acquire a surplus. To sell much and to buy little is the highway to wealth.

Another " free trade fallacy " is, that the reason why articles are produced cheaply in this country with higher wages than rules abroad, is that high priced labor accomplishes much more than low priced—that our mechanics produce enough more to pay for the difference in wages.

It does not appear that the expert mechanics imported from Germany to set up and run the machinery of the Chino Beet Sugar Factory do any more or better work here than they did at home with less wages. And we found that the carpenters did just as good a day's work in Pasadena in 1889 at two dollars per day as they had done in " boom times " for four dollars a day. A good article is always better than a poor one, but it does not make the article better to increase the price.

In our past history, before the tariff question was made the supreme issue, we did not lack for able statesmen to advocate a reasonable, but not prohibitory, protective tariff. Among the ablest of these was James A. Garfield, who expressed himself in Congress as follows :

"We can find ample grounds for the sufficient protection of American manufacturers without distorting the history of our country.

"The decade from 1850 to 1860 was one of peace and general prosperity. If the low tariff and insufficient volume of currency of 1860, caused the alleged distress of that year, how will he account for what he admits, the great distress of 1877, with a much higher tariff and three times the volume of currency of 1860 ?

"Duties should be so high that our manufacturers can fairly compete with the foreign products, but not so high as to enable them to drive out the foreign article and enjoy a monopoly of the trade, and regulate the prices as they please. This is my doctrine of protection."

John A. Logan said in Congress: "When a gentleman stands upon this floor and tells me this high, this extraordinarily high tariff is for protection of laboring men, I tell him that I do not understand how he can substantiate such a theory."

And President Grant, in a message to Congress, referring to the tariff on wool, said :

"All duty paid on such articles (raw materials) goes directly to the cost of the article when manufactured here and must be paid by the consumer. These duties not only come from the consumer at home, but act as a protection to foreign manufacturers in our own and distant markets."

Senator Wilson of Massachusetts said : " Since the reduction of the duties on the raw materials in England, since wool was admitted free, her woolen manufactures

have so increased, so prospered, that the production of
native wool increased more than one hundred per cent.
The experience of England, France and Belgium dem-
onstrates the wisdom of that policy which makes the raw
material duty free."

Protection to wool has been the great inducement with
many farmers to support the high tariff policy.   A farmer
with a small flock of sheep would vote for a high tariff
which cost him every year more than his flock was worth.

The case of the wool tariff is a similar one to that of
the tariff on hides.   The advantage to the leather and
shoe industries and to the country has been so great since
hides were put on the free list as to vastly overbalance
the small gain to the ranch man from the tariff on hides.
We get heavy hides for sole leather from South America
very cheap, and this enables our manufacturers to make
cheap shoes.   In 1871, with a tariff on hides, our exports
of leather amounted to only $2,000,000 in value, while in
1883, with hides on the free list, our exports of leather
amounted to $34,000,000.

Our woolen industries are much hampered by the
tariff on wool.   If our manufacturers could get the cheap,
coarse wools from South America, and other wools which
we can not produce but need in our manufactures, as
cheaply as their foreign rivals buy them, it would give a
great impetus to our woolen industries which are usually
not prosperous, and save the American people millions
of dollars each year.

We now tax the raw material, and pay good prices for
the finished product of English woolen mills, and also in
this way nurse the "shoddy" industry.   But our high
tariff leaders think it necessary to protect wool in order

to keep the farmers on the high tariff side, and to keep
Pennsylvania and Ohio in the Republican column.

Mr. Blaine, as a historian, said : " The tariff of 1846
was yielding abundant revenue, and the business of the
country was in a flourishing condition. Money became
very abundant after the year 1849. Large enterprises
were undertaken, speculation was prevalent, and for a
considerable period the prosperity of the country was
general and apparently genuine. The principles embodied
in the tariff of 1846 seemed for a time to be so entirely
vindicated and approved that resistance to it ceased, not
only among the people, but among the protective economists. So general was this acquiescence that in 1856 a
protective tariff was not suggested or even hinted by any
one of the three parties which presented presidential
candidates."

This period of low tariff continued until after the war
began. A system of high tariff and high taxes was then
instituted as a " war measure." Since the war, those
engaged in the " protected industries " having found that
a high tariff was a good thing for them, have " cried for
more." And so far, like a lot of spoiled children, they
have been getting nearly all they cried for.

PART III.

✛

REMEDIES FOR DEFECTIVE GOVERNMENT, FOR FAULTY EDUCATION, FOR SOCIAL EVILS, FOR BURDENS OF OPPRESSIVE MONOPOLIES AND INEQUITABLE TAXES, AND FOR UNEQUAL DISTRIBUTION AND WASTE OF WEALTH.

CHAPTER XII

MORAL TRAINING IN THE SCHOOLS

In view of the many dishonest and vicious practices which characterize our politics and government, and our social and business life, we are lead to look for a permanent remedy for these great evils; and in doing so find it necessary to go back to first causes and primary principles.

"A fountain can rise no higher than its source." A government can be no better than the governing power. A government by the people will be no better than the people who govern.

The state must again undertake the work of securing a better tone of morality, truth and honor throughout the social fabric, by training the pupils in the schools in such principles.

In the earlier years of the republic the government was administered by men whose rules of conduct were founded upon the decalogue and the golden rule. Stern and exact justice was the order, and purity and honesty of purpose the criterion in the administration of public affairs. Nor was there lack of ability and statesmanship. The faults were mainly errors of judgment through prejudice or defective knowledge, and were usually in defence of that which was deemed to be a just cause, or in opposition to that which was thought to be subversive of good order and of a righteous government.

In those times, as now, religious teaching was the main dependence for training the young in principles of purity and honesty of purpose. Then, religious teaching was accepted as the only source of moral instruction, and was upheld by the state. The Bible was a text book of the school.

In our zeal for maintaining the right of private judgment in matters of religious opinion, and in opposing any tendency to the union of church and state, we have omitted religious teaching in the schools.

But in expunging the Bible from the schools we have made the most serious blunder of not providing anything to take its place as a means of moral training. The whole subject of ethical teaching has been practically relegated to the home and the church.

Much is done by home training, and much by church, Sunday school and other moral agencies to give instruction to the young in principles of virtue and honor; but there remains a great throng of children and youth growing up to manhood and womanhood with little or no instruction in principles of virtue, and much teaching in vice. The state is but an onlooker or silent partner—is neutral or worse. It supplies schools of vice, in saloons and similar agencies, but not schools of virtue. In this, the most vital part of education, that which forms character and determines whether the individual shall become an upright, honorable and useful citizen, or an indifferent or vicious one, the state stands at zero.

It is amazing that we should have gone on in such sublime indifference to this momentous question, leaving wholly to chance or private beneficence a work which should be among the first duties of the state, knowing that but a part, and in some localities a small part of the young are reached by these private agencies.

Some states provide for moral instruction in the schools. Theoretically, perhaps all do. At least they have incorporated in the school law that instruction in good morals and manners shall be given. But, in most cases the state makes no adequate provision for such teaching. It furnishes no text book, adopts no system, lays out no course of instruction. The matter and method are left wholly to the teacher, who may devote a greater or less time to disquisitions on moral philosophy, on historic religions, or on whatever he or she may fancy, provided no religion is taught.

Perhaps this indifference of the people in regard to the question of moral instruction in the schools is partly accounted for by the somewhat prevalent idea and one which has been sometimes promulgated by Christian teachers, that there is no other source of moral teaching, or guide to upright character except the Bible. The church is the great agency for carrying forward moral reforms throughout the civilized world; but it is not always first in such reforms or boldest in their defense; nor does the Bible contain the only embodiment of a moral code. All the principles which go to make right character are fundamental. They depend upon no theological code or form of belief. Religious teaching inculcates these principles, and the church is a potent agency in molding character to an adherence to them. But such principles may be taught and be made effective in forming right character without other influence than that of the teachers and associates who are guided by them.

But we are told that we cannot *form* character in the schools; that we can only *inform* the mind as to what is right and what is wrong—proper or improper, and that the formation of character depends almost wholly upon home training and example and upon one's choice of action through life. As well say that character is not formed by home training as to say it is not formed by school training. Character is formed by all the teaching and all the influences that surround us.

Some children have excellent home training, many have not. In many cases the teaching and associations of the schools have an influence as great as those of the home, and it is the duty of the state to see that that teaching and influence shall be potent in forming right character.

The following marked examples of the *formation* of good character by proper moral training, and even of such formation from the worst classes of subjects, taken from " Moral Education," an excellent work, by Prof. Joseph Rodes Buchanan, show what may be accomplished by such training much better than any argument could possibly do. He says :

" Moral education takes in criminals and turns them out good citizens, by placing them in a moral atmosphere, and keeping them in it till their whole nature is changed, just as men are made criminals by placing them in a criminal atmosphere and keeping them there till they are saturated with baseness."

" One of the most conspicuous examples ever known of the power of moral education in redeeming and elevating criminals was at the Rauhen Haus, near Hamburg, Germany. The place was a prison when Mr. Wichern took charge of it. He threw down the high walls and took away the bars and bolts. He made the children

love him, and he converted them into estimable characters.   Horace Mann says :   " ' The effect attested the almost omnipotent power of generosity and affection.
Children from seven or eight to fifteen or sixteen years
of age, in many of whom early and loathsome vices had
nearly obliterated the stamp of humanity, were trans-
formed not only into useful members of society, but into characters that endeared themselves to all within the
sphere of their acquaintance.'

" We have at this time in the State of Ohio a reform-
atory institution, the State Reform School, near Lancaster, under the management of Mr. G. W. Howe, which
is a wonderful example of what moral power can accomplish.   My first knowledge of this institution was
obtained by meeting Mr. Howe at the Prison Reform
Congress, in St. Louis, in May, 1874.   He told a graphic
story of his labors in attempting to detain and educate
young convicts on an open farm surrounded by the
forest, offering every facility for escape.   His heart sank
in momentary despair and alarm when on a dark night
the boys, having just come from the chapel, started off
with a sudden impulse into the woods, and left him
alone to meditate on disappointments.   It was not long,
however, after their voices had been lost before he heard
them again emerging from the forest, with the cry, 'We've
got him ! We've got him !'   A rough young convict,
recently arrived, thought the dark night offered a fine
opportunity to escape, and started off at full speed.   His
comrades pursued to capture him, and brought him back.
Such was the general sentiment of the school that the
boys would not favor or tolerate running away."

" In this institution none are received but youths convicted of crime.   The report of the board of commissioners for 1868 says :

" ' Of those admitted this year, thirty are under twelve
years of age, and ninety are from eleven to sixteen.
These juvenile offenders are, most of them, charged with
grievous crimes and misdemeanors.   A boy of eleven is

sent for arson; another of twelve for burglary and grand
larceny; and another of fourteen for robbing the United
States Mail. Many of our boys have been the slaves of
the vilest habits and violent passions, of low and debas-
ing propensities. Among our inmates may be found
every shade of character, and every grade of intellect.
The unconquered will, the ungoverned passion, the depraved appetite, with confirmed evil habits, suggest the
difficulties and discouragements in regard to their
reformation.'

" Since the establishment of this reform school, in
1858, about two thousand of these criminal youths have
been received,and all but a very small percentage have been
restored to virtue, having earned an honorable discharge
by good deportment for a sufficient length of time to
satisfy their teachers that they were really reformed."

" The reform school occupies nearly twelve hundred
acres of elevated, hilly, healthy but not productive land,
six miles south of Lancaster, with buildings capable of
accommodating about five hundred boys.

" In this healthy and pleasant home they are received
and managed with unwearied kindness and love, and
carried through a complete course of moral instruction
perhaps the most complete and efficient that has ever
been successfully applied on so large a scale.

" So perfect is the system that, although they receive
so many young criminals from jails, they have no jail,
no prison walls, no bolted gates, but occupy an open farm
in the forest, where the boys are as free as in any
country academy; and are often sent to the village or the
mill on errands, without any guards; and yet there are fewer
escapes than from other institutions where boys are kept
strictly as prisoners within high walls and bolted doors."

" At Lancaster the boys of the school do all the work
on the farm, raising their own food and a large amount
for sale. Every hour is occupied in work, study, moral
instruction, or recreation, leaving no room for evil influences to creep in."

"One of the teachers says :

" As an evidence that our boys are properly controlled, and that they love and honor their home, words of profanity and vulgarity are never heard from their lips; quarrels are unknown; not a seat in the school room, not a wall is defaced by cutting or marking, or soiled by words or pictures of impurity. They are loved and trusted, therefore they are contented, and like good boys stay at home and do their duty. Nor are they held by personal restraint and a system of espionage. For eleven years we have sent almost daily one to six boys with teams to Lancaster, a distance of six miles. Not one of these boys ever betrayed our confidence by escaping, and we never heard a single complaint of bad conduct. Indeed the citizens of Lancaster and the surrounding country have always and uniformly commended their good behavior and gentlemanly bearing."

Such examples, showing what may be accomplished by good moral training in schools, emphasize the demand for such training in all the public schools.

The Kindergarten is an excellent system for training the young. In this way the child is attracted and interested, and the school life begun in a way to produce pleasing and lasting impressions. But a small proportion of children now receive the benefit of this training. It should be made a part of the common school system, and lessons in good morals and good manners should be taught to the youngest pupils, who may be easily impressed with such lessons. And it would be well to carry the Kindergarten Methods of object and oral teaching still farther in the course. We place too much reliance upon text books and too little upon the teacher.

This teaching should be systematic. The state should furnish text books on morals and manners.

Kindness; consideration; *respect for the rights of others*, both in property, person, sensibility and character; truth, honor, honesty; cleanliness, neatness, purity; kindness to animals; industry and frugality; love of home and friends and country; adherence to right principles; advantages of an established character for truth and uprightness; self reliance and self control; courage and fortitude; politeness; these are texts for lessons in moral training, and many of them may be taught to the youngest pupils.

Moral education in the schools must come mainly from the teacher. The text book of ethics must be for the teacher's use, and the teacher must be an exemplification of the lessons to be taught. Courtesy, truth, self control and an earnest desire for the pupil's good, must show forth in the life and the every expression of the teacher to make such teaching effective. *And such kindly virtues must come to be, more and more, indispensible qualifications for the teacher; and the formation and cultivation of such character a prominent part of the normal school work.*

Politeness, which is close akin to kindness, also should be taught constantly and systematically in the schools. Politeness is the outward expression of the kindness which should rule the heart. It is the outward expression of kindness which casts a light across the pathway of others and illumines one's own.

Among Puritans and Quakers we have had examples of an honorable and just character, lacking in outward expressions of kindness; and we still have among their descendants notable examples of this lack of the common courtesies of life, and of the refining influence of such expression. Being of New England parentage, and having felt and observed the need of training in politeness, I can say this without prejudice. The people of the South are noted among Americans for politeness, and as well, for the kindly virtues of consideration and hospitality which politeness indicates.

As one result of the benevolent work of the Woman's Christian Temperance Union, we now have a large part of the youth of the nation taught in the schools the evil results of the use of intoxicating drinks, tobacco and other narcotics, and in this way a foundation is being laid for the final eradication of these evils. This is a beginning of a good work in the schools which should be extended to all other lines of moral instruction. By such systematic training of the young, we may rely upon forming such a character for truth and honor in the large majority of those who are to come upon the stage of action, that it will show forth in the future in a more moral, honorable and benevolent condition of society, and in a more honest, intelligent and economical administration of public affairs.

CHAPTER XIII

A CLEAN BALLOT. CIVIL SERVICE REFORM

The Australian ballot system is an effective remedy for some of our corrupt election practices. It insures freedom, protection and privacy to the voter. It takes away from the rough and vicious element used by dominant parties to carry elections, much of the power they have had over weak, timid, indifferent, ignorant, vacillating and venal voters.

In most of the states this system has been adopted with little opposition. In those states where politics and government are exceptionally pure, as in Michigan and Massachusetts, excellent ballot laws have been adopted, but in states where party management is in bad hands, and where bossism, venality, bribery and corruption are most flagrant—notably in Pennsylvania, New York and California—ballot reform has met with most serious opposition, and defective laws, if any, have been adopted.

As this reform is an effective means for curtailing the power of the party bosses, it has been opposed by the political machines of both old parties. But, notwithstanding this opposition, the general good sense of the people has prevailed and this reform has come to stay. And this fact is one of the most gratifying and hopeful signs of a prospect of improvement in our political life. In the matter of ballot reform it is now only necessary to

have the law extended to other states, and the present
defective laws corrected. So that this question need
trouble us but little. It is no longer a problem.

CIVIL SERVICE REFORM

Of the progress of this reform we cannot say so much.
In this line we are not making much headway. Politicians profess devotion to civil service reform, while their
hearts are far from it. A small number of leaders of both
the old parties are honest advocates of this reform, but
the principal managers of both are upholders and defenders of the spoils system, and both parties are managed in
that way—for the spoils and the plunder. Quay and
Clarkson, both pronounced spoilsmen, have been chair-
men of the republican National committee, and Mr.
Clarkson wrote a magazine article in defense of that
demoralizing system.

Civil service reform has been adopted as a principle of
our government, and its advantages as a potent means of
promoting an honest and efficient administration of the
government business has been fully demonstrated. The
way has been shown, but the dominant parties have
walked not in it—not to any alarming extent ! Theoretically we have adopted the reform, but practically we
have the spoils system as the rule of action in most
departments of the service. In some departments the
civil service rules are fairly well carried out, at least in
the lower appointments. While in other departments
the reform is ignored or but partly adopted.

We cannot expect to make much progress in the adoption of this reform while the leaders of the dominant
parties oppose it. We cannot expect any reform to suc-

ceed when we place it on trial with those who are not in sympathy with it and do not intend to be controlled by it. That is a bad way to "nurse an infant industry." We can hope for the success of any reform, only when the party in power is fully committed to its principles, and pledged to carry it out.

We are not left at all in doubt as to the genuine and complete success and benefit of the merit system in the selection of men for carrying on government business. In most European nations, fitness for the positions, as shown by a thorough examination of candidates, is the requisite in the selection of government employes. In the United Kingdom the administration of the government service is nearly perfect. The candidate must show evidence of good character, must be thoroughly honest and upright, and must be fully qualified and adapted for the position for which he applies. As a result, the British have a model civil service, efficient and painstaking, and mismanagement and peculation are almost unknown.

Time was when the British civil service was as bad as ours has ever been. The king and the nobles gave government places to their favorites, just as our party bosses give government positions to their friends in this country to-day. But the common people in England, to curtail the power of the king and nobility, and to improve the condition of the service, which was bad enough, inaugurated the merit system. When will the common people in the United States curtail the power of the political boss, the politician and the plutocrat (for they work together) by insisting that our government business shall be conducted in the interest of the whole people, and not in the interest of any party or any set of politicians?

The business of the government should be conducted in a business manner. Men should be selected to fill government positions who are in every way fitted and qualified to fill them. We need not hope that any other reform which depends upon government administration can possibly succeed in any full measure until we have a complete reform of our civil service.

Politicians as they enlarge upon the great blessings of our free institutions often talk to us about the " effete monarchies " of Europe. If there is anything "effete" about such monarchies as Prussia, Norway and Sweden, and the United Kingdom, it is not to be found in the conduct of their government service. The term would better apply to the corrupt governments of some of our American cities—New York, San Francisco and Omaha, for example.

Between the governments of British and American cities there is a wide difference in favor of the former. Birmingham, England, and Glasgow, Scotland, may be taken as models of well governed cities. The best, ablest and purest of men are elected to fill important offices, and the mayor and aldermen serve faithfully and without pay, devoting a considerable part of their time in endeavoring to give the best possible government, and to improving the conditions which go to make for the comfort and well being of the people.

CHAPTER XIV

EQUAL SUFFRAGE, EQUAL POLITICAL AND CIVIL RIGHTS

There is no wrong more clearly a wrong ; no imposition more plainly an imposition ; no usurpation of power and authority more decidedly a usurpation, or with less shadow of pretext, than the assumption by man of the sole right to govern ; to make and execute all laws—those which affect woman mainly, as well as those which affect man and woman alike—without the advice, the knowledge or consent of woman. And the many laws made by man which deny to women some of the most common rights, intensify this injustice.

"*Governments derive their just powers from the consent of the governed.*" Since when did woman "consent to be governed ? " Are there any "just powers " of our government, formed and perpetuated with the consent of but one half its people ?

"*Taxation without representation* " is a political outrage, tamely submitted to only by the subjects of absolute monarchs and by people of subject provinces, and often they cry out against it. It was for this outrage that the founders of our Republic declared themselves to be "a free and independent people," and that they would not longer submit to such gross tyranny. Does woman tamely submit to this injustice ? For long years has she solemnly protested against it.

"*All men are by nature free and independent, and have certain inalienable rights,*" among which are life, liberty, and property, and the pursuit of happiness. By the term "men" the Fathers of the Republic certainly meant mankind. But if men have these inalienable rights, have not women an *equal* right to the enjoyment and defence of life, liberty and property ; to the use of all their faculties and endowments ; to the ownership and possession of their labor and the product of their labor and care ; to an equal voice in making and executing the laws and to equal protection under them ?

Governments are instituted among men, not only to protect all citizens in their equal rights, but "*to promote the general welfare.*" How can " the general welfare be promoted " while the most ordinary civil and property rights are abridged and political rights entirely denied to one half the people ?

Established during periods of despotism, feudalism and serfdom, and now rooted, grounded and upheld by long custom, by blind prejudice, and by man's egotism and selfishness, this relic of barbaric times, this vestige of the once "vested right" of man to rule, the denial of political and civil equality to woman, still stands as a landmark of a bygone, savage state, and as a blot on the pages of our present boasted liberty and enlightenment.

During the early and middle ages, woman was looked upon, not only as an inferior, but as a drudge and slave. She was forced to do servile work, chastised and beaten, bought and sold according to the pleasure and caprice of her "lord" and "master." Not that every man was a tyrant, but that woman was subject to his dominion whatever that might be. And this was the case not merely in barbarous countries, but in countries considered civilized, as well. Aristotle held that "The relation of man to woman is that of a governor to a subject." Plato said : "She has only to manage the house well, keeping what there is in it, and obeying her husband."

The women of Sparta and Egypt were held in higher esteem than those of most other countries. Lycurgus said : "Female slaves are good enough to sit at home, weaving and spinning, but who can expect a splendid offspring—from mothers brought up in such occupations?" Yet the free born girl of Sparta was often disposed of in marriage by her father without her consent, and the Spartan husband could bequeath a wife as other property by will, at his death. Under the old Roman law, the husband had absolute power over his wife. He was her sole tribunal.

The Arab bought his wife and treated her as his slave, considering her only as an earthly being. He looked forward to a new wife, resplendent in beauty, in paradise. The Chinaman says a woman has no soul, and the Hindoo widow was burned upon the funeral pile of her husband.

In many savage tribes in modern times, the condition of their women is much as it was a thousand years ago, and it is to a large extent, lamentably true, that, in the most enlightened nations of the present age, woman is still looked upon as an inferior, a dependent, and a drudge; that she is denied many civil and property rights, and that political rights are entirely withheld from her. Does not the ancient view of the proper place of woman correspond in principle with the idea of many men at the present day, who say that woman's "sphere" is at home, washing, mending, cooking, and rearing children ; and that when she seeks other avocations or essays to assist in government, she " loses her womanhood " and " unsexes " herself ?

The common and statute laws of the various states of the Union are based upon the English common law. Here are some of its provisions:

By marriage the legal existence of the woman is " merged in that of her husband." He is her " baron " or " lord," bound to supply her with shelter, food and clothing, and is entitled to her earnings, and the use and custody of her person, which he may seize wherever he may find it.

The husband being bound to provide for his wife, and being responsible for her " morals " and the good order of the household, may choose and govern the domicile, choose her associates, separate her from her relatives, restrain her religious and personal freedom, compel her to cohabit with him, correct her faults by mild means, and if necessary chastise her as though she were his apprentice or child : this being in respect to " the terms of the marriage contract and the infirmity of the sex."

The husband is entitled to recover damages for " criminal conversation with his wife," or for injury to her person whereby he is deprived of his " marital rights," but the wife has no action for injuries to her husband, as she is not entitled to his services or to any separate interest in any thing during her coverture.

The law takes notice only of the injuries done to the " superior of the parties related," because the " inferior has no kind of property in the company, care or assistance of the superior."

In most of the states this common law has been much improved in some particulars, while in other respects, it remains with little or no change. We have such laws as the following:—

By marriage the husband acquires the personal property of the wife, and the rents and profits of her lands, unless otherwise provided for by marriage contract.

The wife has no share in the property of her husband, or in that which they acquire jointly, while they live together.

If the husband die intestate, leaving a widow and issue, the widow has *one-third* of his and their joint personal property, and the *use* of *one-third* of the real estate for life. If there are no children she gets one-half.

If the wife dies without a will, leaving a husband and no children, he gets *all* her personalty, and the *use* of *all* her realty, and *all* their joint estate.

When a divorce is decreed by reason of the wife's adultery, she is entitled to a subsistence out of the property and he gets the balance.

In case of divorce granted on account of the husband's adultery, the wife is entitled to her "thirds" only, and the husband gets the remainder.

In but two states has a woman any legal right to her own legitimate child while she lives with her husband.

A girl at ten years of age (the "age of consent" varies from seven to sixteen years in the different states,) has a legal right to dispose of her virtue and honor to whoever may ensnare her, and the fiend who blasts her young life is held guiltless of offense, but she can not legally dispose of a sheep or an acre of land until she is eighteen.

These examples are sufficient to show the *character* of

existing laws concerning the civil rights of women. *These laws were made by men, without the voice or consent of women, and they show how kind, how generous, how iust, how thoughtful and considerate men have been in guarding and protecting the rights and interests of women!* And yet there are those who think, notwithstanding all this, that women really need to have a voice in protecting their own interests !

Most men are much better than their laws ; yet the majority of men are *not* sufficiently wise, or just, or pure, or unselfish, to make the laws for men and for women also.

Besides, while *the law* makes the husband the owner of the property, in whole or in large part ; while it puts *him* in possession and in the management and control of all the joint earnings and accumulations of property and estate, it necessarily makes the wife a dependent, and subordinate, who must look to her superior to give her from his bounty and reward her from his store.

It is a constant source of humiliation to many women to have to ask their husbands, and often to plead, for provision for the most common necessaries or comforts needed for herself or her household. As the child goes to its parent. so must the wife as a rule go to her husband and ask to be provided for. She must beg for that which of right belongs to her.

Many husbands think themselves very generous to make " presents " to their wives of things they much need. The wife would usually much prefer to receive the money which rightly belongs to her, and make her own selections of articles she needs.

The local preacher who has just received a " donation visit " from members of his flock who think themselves very generous to reinforce the preacher's meager salary and thus lay him under lasting obligation to them, can, in a measure, appreciate the feelings of a wife whose dependent position is made ever present by having to receive donations in lieu of an honest share of the common earnings.

And if this is the case with husbands who are fairly generous and considerate, how will it be with those who are thoughtless, selfish, niggardly ?

There are comparatively very few men who consider this injustice, and accord to the wife, with or without her request, any fair share in the common possession, or any equal voice in its care, its management, and its disposal. And thus it comes about that the wife, as a rule, is but a pensioner, a servant and a beggar, where she should of right be an equal owner and a full partner, and in every respect be consulted, advised and deferred to as such. Men should not speak of *giving* women civil rights. They *belong* to women but have been usurped and withheld by men.

CHAPTER XV.

OBJECTIONS TO EQUAL SUFFRAGE CONSIDERED.

1. *Suffrage is not a right but a privilege.* If so it is a privilege which man grants to himself and denies to woman.

2. *Women are so very different from men.* "They neither think, feel, wish, purpose, will nor act alike."

Is that a reason why men should know better what women need for their comfort and happiness than women themselves know ? Let the women judge what they need.

3. *Women as a rule do not want the ballot.* How do you know that ? You do not submit the question to a vote of women to ascertain.

4. *They do not ask for it.* No other class to whom suffrage has been denied ever asked so much or so persistently for it as have women. They have sent deputations to Congress, to the State legislatures, and to the great conventions of the political parties, many, many times asking for suffrage and remonstrating against the unjust laws made by men which discriminate against women. More than 50,000 women in Massachusetts alone have petitioned for the ballot.

5. *Women have not the physical courage or ability to enforce their will* and therefore are not entitled to the

ballot. Do we select legislators because of physical, or of mental ability ? Is the fact of being defenceless a reason for denying rights to the weak ?

It is true, that women are usually not as strong as men, but this is more the result of habits than of sex. It is not true that there is *naturally* a wide difference in strength and endurance between men and women. Women have strength when they are trained to exercise it, and men do not have strong muscles unless they are developed by use. Women who are inured to labor in the fields and mines in some countries of Europe could much better endure the hardships of a campaign than most professional and business men in our cities. Many of our American women endure as much toil and hardship as do the majority of working men, and they usually work longer hours.

6. *Women have not sufficient mental capacity and force of character to fit them for a share in government.* We find that girls are as good students as boys, and that more of them are graduated from the high schools. And as for force and ability to manage and control affairs we usually find women as competent as men when the occasion demands it. Men do not often show remarkable traits of character until they are called out by force of circumstances. Ulysses S. Grant, as a wood-hauler or clerk in a leather store was no hero.

The history of Europe shows at least as many women as men who have ruled great empires with signal ability, justice and good sense. They have made better rulers than men, more careful and considerate. Maria Theresa, Empress of Austria, found her Empire in a weak and chaotic condition, but she brought order out of confusion

and strength out of weakness.   For forty years she ruled,
loved and respected by her subjects, carefully and ener-
getically attending to all the details of her duties as a
sovereign, and making the Empire a leading power in
Europe.   And in that time she reared a large family of
children, nearly all of whom reached maturity and ably
filled positions of trust and honor.   Frederick, King of
Prussia, said of her "that she exerted a magical power
over her soldiers, and that the Austrian army was never
before so well disciplined and managed."

For over half a century Queen Victoria has ruled over
the most wealthy,and one of the most populous Empires of
the Globe,and no nation has a better or more liberal government.   Victoria recently gave a marked instance of her
good judgment, her high sense of duty and her consideration of the rights of the common people.   When Emperor
William of Germany visited England, he is reported to
have said to her that he thought it would be necessary
for him to declare war upon France, and the Queen re-
plied in part :   "As long as I live I firmly hope that
peace will be maintained.   I am now old, but still feel that
my last years shall not be saddened by more bloodshed
flowing in Europe.   The responsibility which rests upon
you is a terrible one.   It would, in my opinion, be
criminal for any sovereign or statesman to precipitate
events."   And she made it her business to see that war
should be averted.   ·

7. *It would take woman out of her proper "sphere,"*
which is the home; would demoralize her, "bring dis-
credit" upon her ; it would "unsex" her.

Well, if Queen Victoria, and Maria Theresa, and
Queen Elizabeth, and Queen Isabella and hosts of others

could so ably fill high positions as rulers without any such dire results, it will be comparatively safe for an intelligent American woman to undertake to cast a ballot or sit in the jury box without fear of such bad consequences.

Should woman have no aspiration but to keep the house well ? Should the farmer's wife more than the farmer be content with a life filled with a never ceasing round of daily toils ? Should kitchen walls bound her horizon more than the barn-yard fence should that of her husband ?

8. *Why does woman need the ballot ?* She needs it for the same reasons that man does, and because in no other way will equal rights be secured to her. She needs it to protect her rights as a maid, a wife and a mother; to give her " equal pay for equal work," and that she may own her earnings, and be able to own, sell, devise and bequeath her property and estate as she elects.

She needs to be " armed with the ballot" that she may wage effective war against the saloon, the brothel, the gambling den, the political knave, and against all manner of injustice, vice, uncleanness and crime.

She needs it to enlarge her scope of duty, responsibility and usefulness. Woman needs the ballot that she may take her place, and do her part, as man's equal, in instituting new ways and reforms in our methods of government, in devising and shaping legislation, in managing the common interests, in caring for the mutual heritage, and in promoting the general welfare of men *and* women in our common country.

There are, on the other hand, special reasons why women should have the ballot. Women are, as a whole, *better* than men; more moral, more honorable, more sensitive to the wrongs, and more considerate of the rights, of others. Sixty per cent of church members are women; ninety per cent of criminals are men. And, while women would be more merciful to the weak, the needy and the oppressed, they would not be as ready, to permit the oppressor and wrong-doer to escape a just punishment.

Women should largely have the charge and control of the common schools, of reform schools, of almshouses, and of all asylums, charitable institutions, and places of refuge.

No organization of men in the last decade has, in a political or in any other way, accomplished so much for the moral and social betterment of the people of the United States as has the Woman's Christian Temperance Union. It has, almost single handed, introduced scientific temperance instruction in the schools in thirty-seven states. This has been done, mainly through the personal efforts of Mrs. Mary H. Hunt, National Superintendent of Scientific Temperance Instruction of the organization. Mrs. Hunt is one of those remarkable women, who, though hampered by exclusion from political rights, can not be circumscribed in any narrow bounds. We do not know to what extent she has been "unsexed" and "lost her womanhood" by revolving so far from her proper sphere ! She may have suffered very seriously ! But, as the great work she has accomplished for humanity has caused her name to be inscribed high up on the roll of heroes, she can afford to be a martyr in a good cause !

The W. C. T. U. has secured the enactment of laws prohibiting the sale of tobacco to minors in twenty-four states, has succeeded in getting the "age of consent" raised in several states, and has accomplished more in advancing the temperance reform and in abolishing the saloon, than any other agency.

The bare enumeration of these great results attained give little idea of the "toil and endeavor" required to bring about these ends, without political power, or influence. And these facts clearly show that giving political power to women would secure a great moral and social reformation of the people.

The conclusive argument for woman suffrage is, that arguments are not longer needed, if men will but heed the proof of a demonstration. The results of experience in women exercising political rights prove the force of all the arguments advanced in favor of granting them, and show that all the fears and predictions of bad results are groundless.

The English women have had municipal suffrage for twenty years, with such good results that the Lord Mayor of London entertained *thirty-seven total abstinence Mayors* at one time. Fancy the Mayor of Chicago entertaining thirty-seven temperance Mayors! Municipal Suffrage has been extended to the women of Scotland, Ontario, New Brunswick, Nova Scotia and Manitoba. The women of Kansas have had the right of Municipal Suffrage for several years, and have served as city officials in many instances with credit to themselves and good results to the people.

The women of Washington Territory have had full suffrage since 1883, and Chief Justice Greene testifies of the results as follows : "I have now held twelve terms of court in which women have served as grand and petit jurors, and it is certainly a fact beyond dispute that no other twelve terms so salutary for the restraint of crime have ever been held in this Territory." "As to the manner in which the women performed jury duty, I have yet to hear from any one who became qualified to pass an opinion, a single adverse criticism or any word but praise.

In Wyoming, women have had full suffrage for over twenty years. Governor Hoyt said in 1882 :

"Under it we have better laws, better officers, better institutions, better morals, and a higher social condition in general than could otherwise exist. Not one of the predicted evils, such as loss of native delicacy and disturbance of home relations, has followed in its train. The great body of our women, and the best of them, have accepted the elective franchise as a precious boon, and exercise it as a patriotic duty. In a word, after twelve years of happy experience, woman suffrage is so thoroughly rooted and established in the hearts and minds of this people, that among them all, no voice is ever uplifted in protest against or in question of it."

He who starts out seeking any reform in government, asking for himself further privileges or immunities, while utterly ignoring the rights of one-half of the people (and that the *best* half), to a full share with him in all such benefits, is not a reformer or statesman in any just sense, and does not deserve to succeed. He is but a seeker of self-interest, a time-server, or a political and moral coward.

In preparing this chapter I am especially indebted to the work of D. P. Livermore, entitled "Woman Suffrage Defended."

CHAPTER XVI

PROHIBITION OF THE LIQUOR TRAFFIC

The remedies for the drink evil are as patent as the evil itself. In this day and age no search is required to find them. They are published from the housetops.

For the individual the remedy is to "Touch not the cup," and for the state, to abolish the saloon. To find and to perfect the legal remedy has required many years of study and trial, but we now have it in its completeness and success.

Almost every church organization in the land has pronounced in unmistakable terms for total abstinence for the individual, and for prohibition for the state and nation. All the temperance organizations of the country are a unit on this question. From no genuine temperance advocate or body of temperance people does there come any proposition or suggestion or hint of any other remedy for removing the terrible incubus of the drink evil excepting to annihilate the accursed rum traffic.

That a great work has been done and is still carried on in teaching young and old the evils of drink, in inculcating principles and habits of virtue and sobriety, and in properly treating the diseased bodies and depraved appetites of the victims of alcoholic poison, all good people concede. But as a legal remedy, a state and national remedy, it is idle to talk of any other than prohibition of the liquor traffic.

No argument is needed in support of the efficacy of prohibitory laws as a final remedy for the evils of the liquor traffic, except to show the results of the enforcement of such laws ; and we have ample experience to exemplify their utility, and abundance of testimony to prove the good results of this experience.

In 1872, Hon. Wm. P. Frye, then a member of Congress from Maine, sent a letter to Gen. Neal Dow which contained the following :

"Your favor of the 26th inst., containing an inquiry as to the effect of the Maine liquor law in restraining the sale of liquors in our state, etc., is before me ; and in reply, while I am unable to state any exact percentage of decrease in the business,I can and do,from my own personal observation, unhesitatingly affirm that the consumption of intoxicating liquors in Maine is not to-day one-fourth so great as it was twenty years ago ; that in the country portions of the state the sale and use have almost entirely ceased ; that *the law of itself under a vigorous enforcement of its provisions, has created a temperance sentiment which is marvelous and to which opposition is powerless. In my opinion our remarkable reform of to-day is the legitimate child of the law.*" [Italics by the author.]

This letter was endorsed by all the other members of Congress and the two United States Senators from Maine at the time, and by Hon. James G. Blaine, as follows :

James G. Blaine : "I concur in the foregoing statement ; and on the point of the relative amount of the liquors sold at present in Maine and in those states where a system of license prevails. I am sure, from personal knowledge and observation, that the sales are immeasurably less in Maine." In 1882 Mr. Blaine said : "Intemperance has steadily decreased in Maine since the first enactment of the prohibitory law, until now it can be said with truth that there is no equal number of people in the Anglo-Saxon world among whom so small an amount of intoxicating liquors is consumed as among the 650,000 inhabitants of Maine."

Hannibal Hamlin, United States Senator from Maine, and formerly Vice-President of the United States : " I concur in the statements made by Mr. Frye. In the great good produced by the prohibitory liquor law of Maine no man can doubt who has seen its results. It has been of immense value."

Lot M. Morrill, United States Senator from Maine : "I have the honor unhesitatingly to concur in the opinions expressed in the foregoing by my colleague, Hon. Mr. Frye."

John Lynch, member of Congress from Maine : " I fully concur in the statements of my colleague, Mr. Frye, in regard to the effect of the enforcement of the liquor law in the State of Maine."

John A. Peters and Eugene Hale, members of Congress from Maine : " We are satisfied that there is much less intemperance in Maine than formerly, and that the result is largely produced by what is termed prohibitory legislation."

All the governors of Maine for the last twenty-five years have testified to the good results of the enforcement of the prohibitory laws of the state. Here are specimens of their testimony from the continuous line of governors from 1872 to 1888 :

Governor Chamberlain (1872) : "The law is as well executed generally in the state as other criminal laws."

Governor Perham (1872) : "I think it safe to say that it (the volume of the liquor trade) is very much less than before the enactment of the law—probably not one-tenth as large."

Governor Dingley (1874) : " In more than three-fourths

of the state, particularly in the rural sections, open dram-shops are almost unknown and secret sales are comparatively rare."

Governor Conner (1876) : "Maine has a fixed conclusion upon this subject. It is that the sale of intoxicating liquors is an evil of such magnitude that the well being of the state demands that the conditions of the social compact warrants its suppression."

Governor Robie (1885) : "Criminal statistics show that the law has been beneficial in restraining crime, and the number of indictments found against the violators of the law in all our courts and the fines and costs or sentences of imprisonment imposed prove the general willingness of the people to assist in its enforcement."

Governor Bodwell (1887) : "In from three-fourths to four-fifths of the towns of the state the law is well enforced and has practically abolished the sale of spirituous and malt liquors as beverages. In the larger cities and towns, on the seaboard and at railway centers, it has been found more difficult to secure perfect compliance with the law, but it can still be said that at very few points in the state is liquor openly sold."

Governor Marble (1888) : "Prohibition has · closed every distillery and brewery in Maine. The law has greatly diminished the sale and use of intoxicating liquors and increased sobriety and morality among the people, especially outside of the cities. It is certainly the best law of which I have any knowledge, and wherever public sentiment favors its enforcement it works perfectly."

We give below some utterances from some public men of Iowa as to the results of prohibition in that state :

Governor William Larabee (a sturdy opponent of Prohibition before its enactment, but converted into a most ardent supporter after due observation of the workings of the law), in a letter to Rev. William Fuller, of Aberdeen, S. D., Feb. 16, 1889 : "I think more than half of the jails in the state are entirely empty at the present time. There are 98 less convicts in our penitentiaries than there were three years ago,notwithstanding the growth of the population. Expenses in Criminal Courts have decreased very largely during the last few years. ˙ Tramps are very scarce in Iowa. There are evidently very few attractions for them here. Probably more than 3,000 of their recruiting stations have been closed in Iowa during the last five years. The wives and mothers of the state, and especially those of small means are almost unanimously in favor of the law. .The families of laboring men now receive the benefits of the earnings that formerly went to the saloons. There is no question in my mind but what the law is doing good for the people. My views heretofore advanced in favor of the law are strengthened and confirmed by added experience. Our people are more determined than ever to˙make no compromise with the saloons. The law has more friends in the state than it ever had before, and I am satisfied that no state can show results more gratifying."

United States Senator, James F. Wilson, in a letter to the New York *Voice* for Oct. 9, 1890, said : "It gives me pleasure to be able to say that in every desirable aspect of the case prohibition has been beneficial to Iowa. I have a pretty accurate knowledge of the condition existing in Iowa, as induced by prohibition, and I do not hesitate to say that they are all better for its presence than they would have been without it. In the several features of the case as respects business, value of property, moral and educational conditions, diminution of crime and criminal expenses, social and domestic phases of society, Iowa is ready to stand in a row of the states for examination with no fear that any of her sisters will, at the conclusion, stand nearer the head of the line than will she."

J. F. Kennedy, M. D., Secretary of the Iowa State Board of Health, in a letter to the *Voice* of Oct. 9, 1890 :

" In all respects our people have been greatly benefited. Crime and immorality have greatly decreased ; social conditions have improved ; homes have become more home-like, and thrift and the angels of hope have gone into many homes where the blight of poverty and the demon of despair had taken their abode."

W. W. Field, Director of the State Agricultural Society, in a letter to the *Voice* for Oct. 9, 1890 : "I do not mean to say that no liquor is sold and used in the state, but I do say that the quantity is small compared with saloon times, and that our young men are not tempted as formerly, and are being taught that to drink is to lower themselves in the estimation of the best society. It is rare now to see a drunken man upon our streets, and at our recent State Fair, where there were upon our grounds one day 50,000 people, not a man was seen under the influence of liquor."

The State officers of Kansas, nine in number, in 1889, in co-operation with the officers of the State Temperance Union, issued a formal declaration concerning the results of the prohibitory law, in which the following was said in regard to the consumption of drink, etc.:

" The law is efficiently and successfully enforced. The direct results of its enforcement are plain and unmistakable. We believe that not one-tenth of the amount of liquor is now used that was used before the adoption of the prohibition law.

" Our citizens fully realize the happy results of the prohibition of the manufacture and sale of liquor, as these results are seen in the decrease of poverty and wretchedness and crime, and in the promotion of domestic peace and social order—in the advancement of general enterprise and thrift. In our opinion the prohibition law is now stronger with the people than it was when adopted. It has more than met the expectations of its warmest friends. It is steadily winning the confidence and support of thousands who were its bitterest enemies."

Senator John J. Ingalls, in an article in the *Forum* for August, 1889, used the following pithy and forcible language : " Kansas has abolished the saloon. The open dramshop traffic is as extinct as the sale of indulgences. A drunkard is a phenomenon. The barkeeper has joined the troubadour, the crusader and the mound-builder. The brewery, the distillery and the bonded warehouse are known only to the archæologist. Temptation being removed from the young and the infirm, they have been fortified and redeemed. The liquor-seller being proscribed is an outlaw and his vocation is disreputable. Drinking being stigmatized is out of fashion and the consumption of intoxicants has enormously decreased. Intelligent and conservative observers estimate the reduction at 90 per cent.; it can not be less than 75."

Governor John A. Martin (a vigorous opponent of the Prohibitory Amendment when it was first agitated, converted to the cause of prohibition by the results of the law), in his farewell message to the state legislature, January, 1889 : " Fully nine-tenths of the drinking and drunkenness prevalent in Kansas eight years ago has been abolished. * * * Notwithstanding the fact that the population of the state is steadily increasing, the number of criminals confined in our penitentiary is steadily decreasing. Many of our jails are empty, and all showed a marked falling off in the number of prisoners confined. The dockets of our courts are no longer burdened with long lists of criminal cases. In the capital district containing a population of nearly 60,000, not a single criminal case was on the docket when the present term began. The business of the police courts of our larger cities has dwindled to one-fourth of its former proportions, while in cities of the second and third class the occupation of police authorities is practically gone. These suggestions and convincing facts appeal alike to the reason and the conscience of the people. They have reconciled those who doubted the success and silenced those who opposed the policy of prohibiting the liquor traffic."

United States Senator P. B. Plumb (always known as very conservative on the prohibition question) : "That there has been a great diminution in the consumption of liquor and in the consequent drunkenness and crime in the state, as the result of the exclusion of the saloon, is everywhere noted and confessed. In fact, no evidence on this point is more conclusive than that the brewers and distillers are so urgent to have saloons re-established. They are not spending large sums of money in this matter for fun."

J. W. Hamilton, state treasurer, Nov. 24, 1889 : "It is well known to my friends that when the prohibition question was first agitated I was an anti-prohibitionist. I did all in my power to defeat the amendment. I was what they called a Glick re-submissionist. But I was mistaken then. The prohibitory law has my endorsement, not alone because it is the doctrine of my party but because I believe it is right. I do not see how any fair-minded man who has lived in Kansas for the past five years can be otherwise than in favor of the law."

Judge W. C. Webb, April 4, 1890 : "I voted in 1880 against the prohibitory amendment. For four or five years afterwards I thought my opinion as to probable results was likely to be vindicated. But it is not so now. Prohibition has driven out of Kansas the open saloon, and has accomplished a vast deal of good—a thousand-fold more than any license law ever did or ever could. A return to whisky and saloon rule would not bring an additional dollar to the state, nor grow an additional bushel of corn, nor give a single ounce of bread to the hungry, nor clothe the nakedness of a single beggar."

During the Eastern Amendment campaigns of 1889 Mr. W. P. Tomlinson, editor of the *Daily Democrat* of Topeka, was induced to make speeches against prohibition. He ventured to assert that prohibition was a failure, and was quoted as saying that "dives and joints" flourished in Topeka, and that "all the iniquities of secret selling" were "added to the lesser evils of the open traffic." Upon his return to Topeka, Mr. Tomlinson was put under oath by the county attorney, and the following testimony was taken :

Q.   Do you know of the existence of an open saloon in Shawnee county at the present time ?

A.   I do not.

Q.   Do you know of an open saloon in Shawnee county within the past two years ?

A.   No ; I do not.

Q.   Do you know of any secret place in Shawnee county where liquor can be bought by the drink ?

A.   I do not.

There is no lack of testimony in favor of prohibition from public men of Maine, Iowa, Kansas and other states, but this will be sufficient in this connection.

Much of this testimony is taken from "The Encyclopedia of Prohibition."

What more could be added to the force and completeness of this evidence ? *Such an array of witnesses in support of any cause would be ample to fully establish it in any just court or with any honest people.* No candid or well informed man or woman denies the effectiveness of the prohibition remedy for this evil. Only people of the baser sort, those who favor the use of liquors and advocate vice ; or those who are not well informed, being misled by misrepresentations of party papers ; or those who do so for political and party uses, oppose prohibition or advocate any other remedy.

It is true that prohibitory laws will not enforce themselves any better than other criminal laws. It is also true that where prohibitory laws have not been enforced it has been for the reason that the managers of the party in power, or the officials whose sworn duty it was to execute the laws, either or both, were not in sympathy with the law, and, because of political purposes or of vicious or money interests, connived with and upheld the law breakers. This has been the one and only cause of prohibition proving in any case a failure or of not being an entire success.

CHAPTER XVII

NATIONALIZATION OF THE LIQUOR TRAFFIC

This is the new remedy for the evil. Whisky at cost. Remove the temptation to sell, by having the government furnish liquors to all who want at cost.

The contention is that the evil of intemperance is kept up by the incentive of the profits made in the manufacture and sale of the liquors, and that if the incentive to sell liquors is removed the evil will disappear. And there are many good people who have expressed their approval of this new remedy for all the evils of the drink curse. How easy it is to forget the main question in considering one of its incidents. It is a case of trying to cure a disease by treating one of its symptoms.

Among the evils of the use of strong drink are the deadly poison instilled in the veins and the terrible appetite engendered in its victims. Furnishing liquors at cost would not neutralize the poison or lessen the appetite or remove the temptation. It surely would not lessen the quantity used. On the contrary it would increase the consumption of liquors. Reducing the cost of beefsteak, or butter, or blankets, or coffee, or coal, or calico, increases the use of these articles. But there is this difference : people need beefsteaks and butter and it would be good for them to have plenty. They do not need whisky and wine, and the less they use of them the better off they are. If beefsteaks and butter could be furnished at ten cents per pound instead of twenty cents it would tend to build up strong men and women. But furnishing whisky and wine at two cents a glass instead of ten cents would not benefit the drinker or the drinker's family. It would be far better to make the stuff *two dollars* a glass, or *twenty dollars* a glass.

We thought we were through with arguments of this kind. This straw has all been threshed over and over again. *Must we flail it some more?*

Whisky at cost ! If that is the remedy we need, what was the matter with us and our fathers fifty years ago ? What was wrong with Massachusetts, when the people had plenty of good, pure New England rum at a very moderate cost—three cents a glass, and sold at every grocery? Why wasn't Maine vastly better 'off with a good supply of rum, and plenty of jails well filled, and the houses so well ventilated when all they had to do was to just put an old hat or coat into the place where the glass ought to be, when the breeze was too fresh? And now the poor people can't get good rum or brandy any more so handy and cheap as they once could !

And what was the difficulty with old Connecticut, the " Land of Steady Habits," with her cider brandy still in every valley and on every hillside ?   When a hundred brandy factories could be counted from one hilltop ? And when all the good people, preachers, deacons and all, with but few exceptions, used to drink ?   And when drinking was popular and " respectable ? " And when it was not particularly disreputable for gentlemen or ladies to get drunk just occasionally ?   And what was the matter with Ohio where the good old farmer used to lay in twenty or thirty barrels of good cider for winter use when it got " hard ? "

And remember they had *pure* liquors in those times. There was no " incentive " to adulterate them, you know, and besides they didn't know how, and they used it themselves.

And then they had all the adjuncts which come along when people use good pure liquor and can get it real cheap, " at cost " as it were.   They had red eyes, and red noses and red faces, and they had ragged coats and patched trousers, and they used to get drunk and pound their wives and throw the children out of doors, and they had delirium tremens, the genuine article.   They used to have visions of snakes and dragons and imps and devils and fiery furnaces.

Yes, they had a good supply of all these things and a great many more of a similar character, ear marks, signs and tokens of the reign of " rum and brandy at cost."

Besides, we have had a class of pretended temperance advocates who urged that the " doggeries " and " low dives" should be suppressed, and liquors sold only in "respectable" saloons and by men of "good moral character," and under proper restrictions. This new remedy is in the same line only a good deal more so. The proposition is to have the government furnish the liquors to the people, openly and above aboard, and in a respectable and lawful manner, and under proper restrictions— that is, not to minors under a certain age, or to men when drunk, or to those known to habitually abuse their families. The government agent to be of good character and to use due "discretion" in furnishing the liquors. It would seem that a bare statement of the proposition would be sufficient to condemn it in the mind of any true friend of temperance. We must not undertake by law to make vice respectable.

We are told that "The only safe practicable deterrent is the firm restraint of a responsible public officer charged with the duty of proper limitation." (Hon. Henry Winn, in New Nation, for Oct. 31, 1891.) The "practicable deterrent" is in "proper limitation" "to drinking men in quantities not to permit drunkenness." Contemplate the "duty" and "responsibility" of such a public officer to determine the proper "limit" or capacity for liquor which each drinker might safely indulge in ! The officer is empowered to decide for each drinker where virtue ends and vice begins !

We have tried licensing and regulating saloons and gambling houses and brothels, but we have not lessened vice in that way. Now we are to have a new remedy for the drink evil, and the social evil, and the gambling evil. We are to have whisky at cost, and prostitution at cost and gambling at cost, and in this way we are very soon to eliminate and blot out these evils ! Because by removing the incentive of making money from the vices of men and women, we at once relieve vice of its charms and appetite and passion of its force !

No. This will never do. If we want to lessen vice, we must not make the government the agency for license, regulation and supply ; and for making it legitimate, respectable and safe ! We must make it an outlaw. Make it unlawful, disreputable and criminal. We must suppress vice and visit crime with the heavy hand of the law.

CHAPTER XVIII

NATIONAL HIGHWAYS—RAILWAY AND TELE-GRAPH LINES

From ancient times, it has been a first duty of civilized governments, a prime requisite of civilization, to provide roads, bridges and other convenient and adequate means of transit and communication throughout the dominions and from one country to another. The people of one part of a country need the products, the wheat or wool, the cattle or corn, the tools or fabrics, which are produced in other localities, and they need to communicate with the people of other localities, and the problem of how to increase the facilities for interchange of commodities, for

the transmission of intelligence, and the transit of the
people, has always been one that has commanded the
attention of the people and the statesmen of all enlightened nations.   At least it has been the case in other
countries, and was in our own in early days, but our
modern statesman is so profoundly engaged in the consideration of three great problems, namely : 1.   Which
party shall be kept in power,   2. Whether the tariff
shall be raised or lowered, and, 3.   How to properly pro-
mulgate the fact of our unparalleled greatness and prosperity, that they do not deem it worth while to devote
precious time to matters of such trifling import.

The noted Appian Way of the Romans, called the
" Queen of Roads," built over two thousand years ago,
and extending from Rome to Brundusium, was probably
the finest great roadway ever built by man in any age.
The road bed was prepared with great care, rocks were
cut through, small valleys filled, ravines bridged and a
solid foundation made through swamps.   The road was
paved with large blocks of basaltic lava carefully cut and
laid on a bed of concrete.

Among the most remarkable highways of any ancient
people were those built by the Incas of Peru.   They made
roads hundreds of miles in extent, substantially built,
having uniform grades, and traversing high mountain
ranges and wide desert wastes, and with post houses at
stated distances.   These works have been much noted by
historians as indicating a high state of civilization.

In early times in this country our statesmen were
engaged in the work of building canals and post roads,
deeming such works to be of great importance to the
nation. The Erie and Champlain canals, built and operated

by the state of New York, have been a great beneficence, not only to the people of that state, but to the people of many other states.   These works have accomplished much in insuring cheap freights from the west to the seaboard. They have made it possible for many a poor man to have a whole loaf when otherwise he would have had but a half loaf or no bread.   Post roads were built to a limited extent by the nation through trackless forests from one state to another.   Before the war the people of Tennessee and some other states had admirable macadamized roads. These examples show that our people were in times past mindful of "promoting the general welfare" in this respect.

Most European nations are very much in advance of our own in the attention given to the public interests in providing good highways for public use and benefit. They usually have much better turnpike roads than we do, and their railways are usually either owned or managed by the government or are under strict government control.   But the people of Australia lead all other countries in the matter of managing their railways in the interests of the people.

To provide public highways, convenient and suitable for all, built for the use and benefit of all the people, and made as nearly free as possible, is a province of government which demands constant attention and should never be lost sight of.

Justice Bradley, of the United States Supreme Court states the well recognized principle of national law in regard to highways as follows :—

"When a railroad is chartered it is for the purpose of *performing a duty which belongs to the state itself.* It is the duty and prerogative of the state to provide means of intercommunication between one part of its territory and another." Also the court has held : "It has never been considered of any importance that the road was built by the agency of a private corporation. No matter who is the agent, *the function performed is that of the state."*

Time was when the turnpike road was the great highway, but that is all changed. Now the railway track is the great highway, and the telegraph wire the swift messenger. The "main traveled road" is comparatively a by-way.

It is true that the railway has been a wonderful means for the advancement of civilization. It has made many things possible and easy which otherwise would be impossible or very difficult. From wide distances it brings the ore to the furnace, the wheat to the mill, the fleece to the factory. It climbs mountains, leaps chasms, and glides over boundless plains and wide rivers with ease and safety. It gives value to the distant mine and valley and forest.

It is true that the telegraph has been a marvelous power for disseminating intelligence through the length and breadth of the land. It gathers the story of great events, the currents of mighty thought and action, and sends them on the wings of the morning. It makes possible the modern great daily newspaper, telling of the exploits and achievements of men in the far corners of the earth.

It is also true that the common people do not derive the benefit from these great agencies which they should do or might do if managed for the people and in their interest. They are not made public highways in a proper sense, but are monopolies over which the nation has very little control. The people have a right to expect and to demand and receive a full measure of advantage from these agencies. And it is the duty of the government to secure such advantage for them. *That this can not be done without government ownership and management is a fact which is slowly but surely dawning upon the minds of the American people.*

The unjust and dishonest management of railway properties, the exorbitant charges, the vexatious discriminations and the waste and loss of the present system, forms one of the greatest burdens upon the people of this country. And not this alone, but the fact that the railway interests are becoming more and more powerful in controlling and disturbing financial and business affairs, in dictating legislation and in corrupting the fountains and defeating the ends of justice, that makes them a menace and danger to the usefulness and perpetuity of our free institutions.

The railways are getting bigger than the government— that is, more powerful. They can spend more money in controlling legislation, in employing able and unscrupulous lawyers and agents to oppose the people's interests and defeat the ends of justice, than the people have to use in any effort to control and regulate them.

The Goulds, Vanderbilts, Huntingtons and Dillons, vastly more than the Carnegies, Rockefellers, Spreckles and all the other plutocrats, are the masters we should fear. Their rules of propriety and justice are to "charge what the traffic will bear," and "the public be damned." In modern railway management as in modern politics " the Decalogue and the Golden Rule have no place." *In no other field for monopolies or combines is there such room for extensive jobbery and plunder. By their devices and manipulations of great properties and interests they are able to divert the flow of a large part of the nation's wealth from its proper channels into their coffers.*

CHAPTER XIX

METHODS OF CONSTRUCTING AND CAPITALIZING RAILWAYS

No man on the outside can know all the "ways that are dark and the tricks that are vain" of the railway schemer, but there are some things that a "wayfaring man" may know. In a general way, here is a history of many ordinary cases of railway construction and capitalization.

There appeared to be a demand for a new line of railroad, or room for another line. A company was organized in the interest of a certain corporation, but which was not known in the new company. There were some local directors and the old company was represented by men duly selected who were to manage and control.

Then the agents and "hustlers" of the company went along the line and held public meetings. They had good speakers, and the importance of railroads in building up a country was not under-estimated. Town Councils and County Commissioners were urged to bear a hand. The company must have free right of way and depot grounds and must have enough bonds and stock subscribed on the line to at least grade the road. Every "public spirited citizen" was expected to take a good block of stock. Solicitors were employed who would double discount any real estate man, insurance agent or lightning-rod peddler!

If the line, by a moderate detour, could be made to

strike either of two rival towns, they were put upon their
mettle. The one which "secured the road" was to
rapidly become a great city, while that which was "left
out in the cold" was soon to be a "howling waste." In
like manner opposite sides of each town were put in active
competition for the coveted prize ; it being shown that
close to the depot would be the chosen place for all the
fine dry goods and fancy stores and the banks ! Why, a
railroad craze is nearly as bad as a boom.

The road being built was operated for a year or two
without paying any dividends. The schemers did not
care to have the balance sheet make any showing of
profit. The farmers found the stock was poor property.
Then the men who were managing the deal watched for a
favorable opportunity, when stocks were low and business
dull, to buy up the out-lying stock at as low a price as
possible. If the game was large enough and the company
strong enough they brought to bear all the power at command to depress the market and produce a condition
favorable for buying at a small price. They then improved
the property, perhaps made some new connecting line
which enhanced its value, and waiting for the right opportunity, re-organized, incorporating two or more lines in
the new company. They "capitalized it"—that is placed
the total par value of the stock—at as high a figure as
they thought it would bear, say fifty or one hundred or
two hundred per cent above the original cost. The stock
and bonds were sold to people who had money to invest
in such "railroad securities." The manipulators bought
in the stock at say fifty or forty or thirty cents on the
dollar of original cost, and they sold at one hundred and
fifty or two hundred or three hundred cents on the dollar.

And this is "profits of constructing and capitalizing." And they take occasion to re-organize whenever suitable opportunity offers.

Sometimes roads are capitalized at five times the original cost. Mr. C. Wood Davis, in his excellent article entitled "Should the Nation Own the Railways," in the *Arena* for July and August, 1891, states that the Kansas Midland, costing but $10,200 per mile is capitalized at $53,000, and that Mr. Gould has managed to float the securities of the St. Louis and Iron Mountain Railway, costing about $11,000 at $55,000 per mile.

It is in such ways that the railway "manipulator" is able to pocket a sum equal to or greater than the entire value of a railway line, in making one big deal. And by such means they become multi-millionaires, money kings, and financial rulers of the nation. Of course, it is all wrong to speak of this, because Mr. Dillon says that "a citizen, simply as a citizen, commits an impertinence when he questions the right of a corporation to capitalize its properties at any sum whatever."

The manipulators having made a "ten strike" in constructing and capitalizing at high values, endeavor to make the roads pay dividends on the watered stock. If the property is poor, the big operator, looking for a favorable opportunity, unloads his stock which is no longer a source of revenue, and seeks new fields for investment and profit. He turns off his lean stock at as good a price as possible, and hunts some fat stock that can be bought low and multiplied.

There are also in the ordinary field of the great operator other ways whereby he is able to take care of himself before providing interest to bondholders or dividends on stock. There are high salaries for the chief and his friends; big commissions to brokers and soliciting agents which will bear a " divide ;" low rates of freight given to personal agents or friends and profits of the short rate divided between the official and shipper, and other ways, some of which will be considered.

CHAPTER XX

FOUR REASONS FOR NATIONAL OWNERSHIP OF RAILWAYS

Some of the many reasons why the nation should own the railways ; the corrupting influences and practices under our present system upon legislation and the action of the courts ; the dangers to our financial and business interests from the railway money power ; the many unjust discriminations under present management ; the savings which can be made in many ways in managing and operating the roads and the increased safety and security to life and property which may be obtained by national ownership, are enumerated under twenty-four heads, as follows, in this and two following chapters.

1. *The corrupting influences of present railway management upon elections, legislation and the courts.*

Under this head we have the use of stocks, bonds, money and passes to influence legislators, commissioners,

judges and jurymen. This has been done in state and
national legislation, and in cases in the courts where the
railway companies have sought to defeat the ends of justice. One of the best known cases is the notorious
" Credit-Mobilier " scandal, in which the stock of the
Union Pacific Railroad was used in Congress to secure
legislation favorable to the company in constructing and
obtaining subsidies and also to secure the acceptance of
sections of the road which were not built according to
the requirements of government.

Mr. F. B. Thurber, in an article entitled " The Railroads
and the People," in *Scribner's Magazine* of December,
1880, gives instances in this line as follows : Mr. Jay
Gould, in giving his evidence before a committee of the
New York legislature, which was examining the affairs of
the Erie Railroad in 1873, stated as follows :—

"I do not know how much I paid toward helping
friendly men. We had four states to look after, and we
had to suit our politics to circumstances. In a democratic district I was a democrat ; in a republican district
I was a republican, and in a doubtful district I was
doubtful ; but in every district and at all times I have
been an Erie man."

The committee stated in their report as follows : " It
is further in evidence that it has been the custom of the
managers of the Erie Railway, from year to year in the
past, to spend large sums to control elections and to
influence legislation. Mr. Gould admitted the payment
of large sums to influence legislation. The memory of
this witness was very defective as to details, and he could
only remember large transactions ; but could distinctly
recall that he had been in the habit of sending money
into the numerous districts all over the state, either to
control nominations or elections for senators and members

of Assembly.   He considered that, as a rule, such investments paid better than to wait till the men got to Albany,
and added the significant remark, when asked a question,
that 'it would be as impossible to specify the numerous
instances as it would to recall to mind the numerous
freight cars sent over the Erie road from day to day.'
It is not reasonable to suppose that the Erie railway has
been alone in the corrupt use of money for the purposes
named ; but the sudden revolution in the direction of this
company has laid bare a chapter in the secret history of
railroad management such as has not been permitted
before.   It exposes the reckless and prodigal use of money
wrung from the people to purchase the election of the
people's representatives, and to bribe them when in
office."

Mr. James Parton stated in a lecture : " Men who
bribe and are bribed nowadays talk about the matter
without a blush.   An officer of the New Jersey Legislature told me how the bribing was done, and how he did
it himself.   The railroad man said to him, 'Come to my
room at eight o'clock this evening,' and when the farmer-
legislator got there the railroad man said : ' By the way,
Mr. Smith, you did not call upon us to subscribe toward
the expenses of your election.   I know it must have cost
you a great deal, and, better late than never, here is
something toward it,' and the railroad man passed over a
pile of money much more than the farmer's election
expenses.   ' I know', added the corruptionist, by way of
casual remark, 'that you would not vote for any bill that
would not be good and honest, but there is a bill of ours
now before your house that, you will take my word for it,
is for the best interests of the community; examine it,
and if you conscientiously think so, too, of course you
will vote for it.' "

In 1880 the New York Board of Trade and Transportation published a report in which they most forcibly stated
the case as follows :—

" Honestly and equitably managed railroads are
the most beneficent discovery of the century, but
perverted by irresponsible and uncontrolled corporate
management, in which stock-watering and kindred
swindles are tolerated, and favoritism in charges is permitted, *they become simply great engines to accomplish
unequal taxation, and to arbitrarily redistribute the wealth
of the country. When this state of things is sought to be
perpetuated by acquiring political power and shaping legislation through corrupt use of money, the situation grows more
serious.*"

A committee of the New York Chamber of Commerce
made a report to that body in 1880 in which they used
language as follows :—

" We cannot uphold a system of operating public highways which is honey-combed with abuses and which is
controlled absolutely by a few individuals who tax production and commerce at will, and who practically dictate
what reward the producer, manufacturer, and merchant
shall secure for his labor."

Messrs. Gould and Dillon now ask of Congress a farther
extension of the mortgage indebtedness of the Union and
Central Pacific roads, of which debts they propose to pay
no part, either principal or interest, but ask for an extension of a hundred years at a rate of one and one-half per
cent interest. It does not seem possible that any man in
Congress could labor for such a proposition with very
much zeal unless he were " influenced " to do so by some
potent incentive.

2. *National ownership of railroads would bring to an end
the power which the great railroad managers have over the
financial and business affairs of the country.* They could no
longer wreck railways, plunder shareholders and precipitate financial disasters.

* " In 1874, the Senate of the United States, in response to a general demand, appointed a special committee on transportation, composed of Senators William Windom, of Minnesota ; John Sherman, of Ohio ; Roscoe Conkling, of New York ; H. G. Davis, of West Virginia ; T. M. Norwood, of Georgia ; J. W. Johnson, of Virginia ; John H. Michell, of Oregon, and S. B. Conover, of Florida. The committee occupied the entire summer of 1874 in making an exhaustive examination of the subject, and in their report we find the following :—

" In the matter of taxation, there are to-day four men representing the four great trunk lines between Chicago and New York, who possess, and who not infrequently exercise, powers which the Congress of the United States would not venture to exert. They may at any time, and for any reason satisfactory to themselves, by a single stroke of the pen, reduce the value of the property in this country by hundreds of millions of dollars. An additional charge of five cents per bushel on the transportation of cereals would have been equivalent to a tax of forty-five millions of dollars on the crop of 1873. No Congress would dare to exercise so vast a power except upon a necessity of the most imperative nature ; and yet these gentlemen exercise it whenever it suits their supreme will and pleasure, without explanation or apology. With the rapid and inevitable progress of combination and consolidation, these colossal organizations are daily becoming stronger and more imperious. *The day is not distant, if it has not already arrived, when it will be the duty of the statesman to inquire whether there is less danger in leaving the property and industrial interests of the people thus wholly at the mercy of a few men, who recognize no responsibility but to their stockholders, and no principle of action*

---

* This is copied from a valuable article, entitled " The Railroads and the People " by F. B. Thurber, in Scribner's Magazine for December, 1880. (The italics are the author's.)

but personal and corporate aggrandizement, than in adding
somewhat to the power and patronage of a government
directly responsible to the people and entirely under their
control. Report of the United States Senate Committee
on Transportation Routes, page 158."

The dangerous power which could be wielded by a combination of two or more unscrupulous railway kings, to
depress values and jeopardize the financial interests of the
country in order to get control of coveted properties, can
not be contemplated by any patriotic citizen without
fearing the most disastrous consequences. There are
times of depression in business, when we have short crops
and foreign nations have plenty and the balance of trade
is against us ; when we have had floods and frosts and
drouths ; when chinch bugs and army worms have
devoured ; when the farmer has little ready money and
the hum from the factory is silenced ; when the merchant's
goods remain useless on his shelves and when men feel
that but one more straw is needed to break the camel's
back. Then is the favored opportunity of the railroad
wrecker. In order to gain his selfish ends and add still more
to his illgotten and useless wealth, he stops at no calamity
which might befall the people as a result of his inordinate
greed. Though tens of thousands go supperless or home-
less or unsheltered from the storm, matters not to him.

3. *National Ownership would stop the "pass" evil.* People
who rode on railways would all have to buy tickets.
There would be no " dead heads." The rich would have
to pay as well as the poor. Notwithstanding laws to the
contrary, it is estimated that fully ten per cent of railway
travel goes without pay. Passes are given whenever it
seems to the interest of the companies, for the purpose of

influencing government officials who have any power to favor the companies, to newspaper men, to railway men and officials and their relatives and friends, to large shippers, to those who seem to have political power and influence, and often for no good purpose.

From whatever cause granted they are a tax upon the roads which in the end must be paid by the people who use the roads.

4. *There would be no high capitalizing*, and opportunities for multi-millionaires to scoop in the wealth of the people by millions in one big deal would not be so plentiful as now. In no other way possible can the millionaire amass wealth so rapidly as by this scheme of manipulating railway securities. If the Goulds and Dillons— the "dangerous wealthy classes"—*are* a danger and a menace to the welfare and stability of popular government and a drain upon the wealth of the people, (and what well informed man does not know that they are,) then here is the place, more than any other place, to begin to buttress, to build breakwaters and seawalls to oppose this dangerous power and protect the interests of the American people.

Mr. Sidney Dillon, President of the Union Pacific Railway, in his article on "The West and the Railroads" in the *North American Review* for April, 1891, in which he speaks at length of the advantages which the railways have been to the country, goes on to say: —

"Grave charges are made : as, for instance, that the roads have in numerous instances been fraudulently over-capitalized and excessively loaded with bonded debt ; that they monopolize traffic ; that they charge unjust rates of freight in order to pay dividends on fictitious

values of stock ; that they favor one class of shippers at
the expense of another class ; that they permit the
accumulation of unreasonably large fortunes, and, to use
a favorite phrase of demagogic orators, constantly ' tend
to make the rich richer and the poor poorer.'

" Legislation has been called in to give force to the
theories involved in these declarations, particularly in
the states west of the Mississippi, which happen to be
the communities that owe their birth, existence, and
prosperity to these very railways.   Statutory enact-
ments interfere with the business of the railway,
even to the minute details, and always to its detriment.
This sort of legislation proceeds on the theory that the
railroad is a public enemy ; that it has its origin in the
selfish desire of a company of men to make money out of
the public ; that it will destroy the public unless it
is kept within bounds ; and that it is impossible to
enact too many laws tending to restrain the monster.
The advocates of these statutes may not state their
theory in these exact words ; but these words certainly
embody their theory, if they have any theory at all beyond
such prejudices as are born of the marriage between ignorance and demagogism.

" Many of the grievances that are urged against railways are too puerile to be seriously noticed, but the
reader will pardon a few words as to ' over-capitalization.'
Now it is impossible to estimate in advance the productive power of this useful and untiring servant.   Sometimes
a railway is capitalized too largely and then it pays
smaller dividends ; sometimes not largely enough, and
then the dividends are much in excess of the usual interest
of money."

(That is to say, that the aim is to capitalize them at
such a figure that the stock will pay only a fair interest
on the investment. If capitalized at actual cost the
present charges would show too large gains. Appearances
must be considered.   Author.)

" In the former case stockholders are willing to reduce the face of their shares, or wait until increase of population increases revenue ; in the latter they accept an enlarged issue.   But, as a matter of reason and principle, the question of capitalization concerns the stockholders and the stockholders only.   *A citizen, simply as a citizen, commits an impertinence when he questions the right of any corporation to capitalize its properties at any sum whatever. That any railway anywhere in a republic, should be a mon opoly, is not a supposable case.*"

CHAPTER XXI

FIFTEEN REASONS FOR NATIONAL OWNERSHIP OF RAILWAYS.

5. *Government Ownership would stop unjust discriminations,* by the use of which, like the pass evil, one class of people or one locality is favored at the expense of others.   There are many ways of discriminating, some of which will be considered in another place.   The most common discrimination is against points where there is no opportunity for competition, shippers being charged higher rates at such points than over the same roads for longer distances where there is a competing line.   This is one of the most common complaints against the roads. To endeavor to remedy such evils as this we have state legislation, the interstate commerce law of congress, and state and national commissions.   But all such efforts are, in the main, futile.   These laws are constantly evaded in one way and another, and without national ownership of the roads this evil will continue.

"The testimony in the Pennsylvania investigation showed that the trunk lines of railroads paid in rebates to the Standard Oil Company, within the period of eighteen months $10,151,218. In a report to the New York Chamber of Commerce, the Committee on Railroad Transportation of that body alludes to this subject as follows : —

" How oblivious of their obligations as common carriers, and how regardless of public rights, are the great trunk lines, is illustrated by their making an agreement with the Standard Oil Company (Article 4) to protect them 'against loss or injury from competition.' What has happened in the case of the Standard Oil Company may happen in other lines of business. With the favor of the managers of the trunk lines, what is to prevent commerce in the rest of the great staples from being monopolized in a similar manner ? Already, indeed, it is taking this course. One or two firms in Baltimore, Philadelphia, New York and Boston, with their branch houses in the West, are, by the favor of the railroads, fast monopolizing the export trade in wheat, corn, cattle, and provisions, driving their competitors to the wall with absolute certainty, breaking down and crushing out the energy and enterprise of the many for the benefit of the favored few."*

We now come to consider some of the savings which might be effected by national ownership in the ordinary operating expenses of the roads.

6. *Most of the cost of advertising would be saved.* A large amount of money is constantly being expended by the various companies in advertising the advantages of their lines. This is done in newspapers and periodicals, and by books, pamphlets, circulars, maps, chromos, etc. All of these expenses except such as is necessary in advertising the running of trains, probably ninety per

(* From article of Mr. F. B. Thurber, in *Scribner's* of December, 1880.)

cent of the whole amount, would be unnecessary under national ownership. There would be no more occasion for advertising any advantage of particular lines of railway, than there now is of advertising the advantages of any particular mail route by the government. Traffic and travel would then seek the shortest or most convenient route, without expending large sums of money in trying to send it some other way.

7. *The entire cost of soliciting traffic and travel would be saved.* Each company now employs soliciting agents, gives commissions to the local agents of other roads for sale of tickets, pays commissions to brokers for securing freights, maintains expensive special ticket and freight offices off its lines, and in many other ways spends money to secure business. This would all be saved and would mean cheaper railroad rates.

8. *It would relieve the railroad business of the burden of the sixty-eight Traffic Associations.* This institution is the " Combine " and regulator between several companies. They employ a high-priced manager with a full corps of assistants, and they require a central location in a large city with commodious and well appointed offices. The manager is the umpire who regulates the proportion and direction of traffic going over the different lines. It is a combine to keep up rates, to send the farmer's products over the longest lines, to get as much money as possible out of the public, and to endeavor to fairly distribute the spoils between the combining companies.

9. *All legal expenses would be saved.* Under this head are salaries of attorneys and their assistants, and sums paid to legislators, judges and other officials to "influence" legislation and corrupt the sources of justice. The ablest

attorneys are employed, and higher salaries paid than are received by any judges upon the bench. They also have use for a company of lobbyists, bribers and attorneys and others "to do the dirty work." The companies have many uses for able attorneys ; to secure nominations by the political parties of men who are favorable to the railway interests and to work for their election ; to have an oversight of legislation ; to secure the passage or repeal of laws in the railway interest ; to assist judges and commissioners in properly "construing" laws which they cannot otherwise abrogate ; to see that the interests of the corporation are not infringed upon by other companies ; to make the most of the "law's delays" and to make all the use possible of the many tricks and devices which may be resorted to to wear out the patience and exhaust the resources of those who have the hardihood to contend with one of these giant corporations. They have political influence ; they have long purses ; they are fully armed and equipped for any legal contest ; they never get tired, never grow old, never die, never lose their grip, and they are in business for what is in it for themselves.

It is true, that under present conditions there is a legitimate use for railway attorneys, but in the main the money expended under the head of "legal expenses" and what Mr. Gould called the "India rubber account," is used to corrupt the fountains and defeat the ends of justice. The Australian railways, which are built, owned and managed by the state, are operated directly in the interests of the people and without the expenditure of a single dollar for legal expenses.

During the war the national government, under the sys-

tem of war taxes, collected from the New York Central
Railroad company a half million dollars. The company
claimed that the tax was not authorized and employed
Mr. Roscoe Conkling to bring suit to compel the government to refund the money. Mr. Conkling was at that
time United States Senator, and political boss of the
republican party of the State of New York, and he
appeared as counsel for the company in the court at
Canandaugua to try the case, opposed by a District Attorney who was counsel for the government and before a
judge who made the charge to the jury, both of whom
owed their official existence to Mr. Conkling. The company recovered the half million dollars.

10. *It would save about ninety-five per cent of the present
cost of high salaried officials and expensive offices.* There
are about five hundred railway companies, each of which
has its president, vice-president, general manager, general
freight agent, general passenger agent, auditor, treasurer,
and other officials, with assistants, and a full corps of
secretaries, clerks, book-keepers, etc. And this calls for
expensive general headquarters, which are often off the
main line in some large city, and so placed as to assist
in advertising the road and where proper attention can be
given to exercising an influence on the value of stocks,
either in raising or depressing them. The total of this vast
expenditure of money is a very large sum compared with
what it would cost to oversee the operating of the roads
under economic national ownership.

11. *It would save a large expenditure in book-keeping.*
There are accounts of freights and fares sent over different
lines on pro rata charges which must be credited up to
the separate roads, accounts of all the officials and com-

plex machinery of management under the present system, none of which would be required under national ownership.

12. *There would be a large reduction in local offices and officials.* Now each company has its local ticket and freight office, its yards and switches, with the necessary complement of officers and men at each station. Under national ownership, all trains would run to central depots and in most cities but one complement of offices and officials and yards would be required. The railway business would be simplified just as the mail business is now. And there would be no hack transfers from one depot to another to vex the tired traveler.

13. *It would give us uniform rates,* on all lines and everywhere, instead of the vexatious, irregular, uncertain, discriminating rates of freights and fares under present management.

14. *It would give us a reduction of freight rates and fares to a legitimate business basis.* This would be made possible by cutting off the many leaks caused by extravagance, jobbery, loss and waste under the present system, and by giving to the people a large part of the stealings and profits which now go to the railway officials or to the shareholders. Passenger fares on the Austrian railways are about forty per cent of what they are with us. Where the Hungarian railways formerly carried two passengers at one and a half cents per mile, they now carry five at three-fourths of a cent per mile. They have uniform rates under what they term the "zone system," which makes a unit rate for every te. miles or fraction of ten. The large reduction in rates which would be made possible by national ownership would be a vast saving

to the people of this country, and travel would be greatly increased. There are no exceptions to a rule of this kind— that use increases as price decreases. Under national management when properly organized we may reasonably expect a reduction of fifty per cent in the cost of transportation.

Prof. Arthur L. Hadley in his article in the *Forum* for April, 1891, on " Railway Passenger Rates," in which he argues that we already have good and cheap passenger service and that rates can not be much reduced without working a hardship to the companies, says: " The assumption so frequently made, that a reduction in rates would cause an enormous increase in travel in this country, is for the most part a pure assumption, not borne out by the facts." That is poor special pleading. That a reduction in the cost of *anything* which the people need and can not well afford to buy, is followed by a *corresponding* increase in the amount used, is a fact so well known that it is useless for anyone to deny it. And the use of such an argument in trying to defend the present monopolies shows the dearth of reasons for maintaining the present plundering and wasteful railway *regime.*

15. *There would be a large saving in the cost of our mail service.* The nation now pays the railway corporations large sums for transporting the mails, and with the railways owned by the government the people would gain what profits there is to the companies in this transportation.

16. *It would absorb the express business.* The nation now does a parcel delivery business in connection with the mail service, which is very much cheaper, for articles which may be admitted in the mails, than express

charges. The government could readily undertake to do all kinds of express business as a part of the postal system and to do it with celerity and security, and vastly cheaper than it is now done by express.

The express business is a vast monopoly added to the railway monopoly. The express companies pay the railway companies a profit on the cost of hauling express cars and then make immense profits out of their business. The United States Express Company, the Adams Express Company and Wells, Fargo & Co. are cormorants whose heads would be cut off by national ownership of the railways.

17. *There would no longer be a scarcity of cars* to do the business of the country. There are railways which have been wrecked or plundered by the managers, which are very poorly equipped, and others where high salaries and good dividends to shareholders have been paid at the expénse of providing a proper supply of rolling stock. Again, when cars are scarce it gives an excuse to officials to favor their own business agents, or shippers with whom they are interested, being short when others need cars. And a great saving would be effected in this connection by using cars on lines where for the time or season there was the most business, as in handling the wheat, corn, cattle, hogs, oranges, etc., at times when those commodities needed to be moved, and when on other lines there was not as much demand for cars.

18. *It would save the expense of useless parallel lines.* In many cases roads have been built for considerable distances paralelling other lines. Each company must have its complete through line, and so we have thousands of miles of railways running through the same territory

and competing for the same trade. The constructing and
operating of these roads has been an added expense to the
cost of transport. While localities have been benefited
by such competition, in the end the cost comes out of the
people. The nation would not need some of these lines
unless to form double track routes.

19. *Traffic would go by the shortest route.* Now passengers and freight are often sent by a round-about way,
either to secure business by competing roads or under the
regulation of traffic associations. This shows that if one
line can afford to haul a car of freight 800 miles for a
certain price, the line which gets the same money for
hauling the same freight but 600 miles is making an
exorbitant charge. Also in the same line there are
unnecessary long hauls dictated by companies to whose
interest it is to haul as far as possible over their own
lines, or by traffic managers to secure as much business
as possible for their associations.

CHAPTER XXII

FIVE REASONS FOR NATIONAL OWNERSHIP OF RAILWAYS

20. *There would be more safeguards for the security of life and property,* more guards at street crossings, more interlocking plants at crossings of railway lines, better appliances for heating and lighting, and in short more consideration for the health, comfort and convenience of the traveling public. Because the roads would be run for the benefit of the people, and their interest would be paramount to all others. These facts are demonstrated by experience in the Australian railways, which are managed by the government, where there is a much less proportion of casualties than in the United States.

21. Besides the more common or better known ways and schemes of the railway corporations or their managers for gaining power and wealth, there are other fields which they enter, and other lines of business in which they engage. Wherever the railway takes up a line of business those with whom they compete may as well give it up at once, for they will find it a losing game. Nobody can compete with a railway corporation while it uses its power to build up its own business by destroying that of its rivals. In these outside lines of business the companies often become very oppressive and aggravating.

Sometimes the companies carry on these added lines of

business directly, but more commonly under some other firm or corporate name. Often officials of the companies undertake outside lines of business, either employing agents, or sharing profits with some man or firm already in business, or organizing companies for the purpose. Here are some of the kinds of business in which they engage : *they build towns and cities,* using lands that are given them or buying lands for the purpose, and using the power of the company to build them up by discriminating against other localities so as to throw as much business as possible to the new town.   This comes in as a part of the profits of the railway construction, and large sums are made in this way.

22. *They buy coal fields and to a large extent monopolize the coal trade.* Most of the valuable coal fields of the country are owned by the railways or railway officials. Their exactions from consumers of coal, and their discriminations against other mine owners and shippers, have often been very oppressive and burdensome.   Mr. C. Wood Davis, in his excellent article in the *Arena* for July and August, 1891, gives instances of this as follows :

"Under corporate control, railways and their officials have taken possession of the majority of the mines which furnish the fuel so necessary to domestic and industrial life, and there are but few coal fields where they do not fix the price at which so essential an article shall be sold, and the whole nation is thus forced to pay undue tribute.

"Controlling rates and the distribution of cars, railway officials have driven nearly all the mine owners who have not railways or railway officials for partners, to the wall.   For instance in Eastern Kansas, on the line of the St. Louis and San Francisco Railway Company, were two coal companies, whose plants were of about equal capacity, and several individual shippers.   The railway company and its officials became interested in one of the coal companies, and such company was, by the rebate and other processes, given rates which averaged but forty per cent of the rates charged other shippers, the result being that all the other shippers were driven out of the business, a part of them being hopelessly ruined before giving up the struggle. In addition to gross discriminations in rates this railway company practised worse discriminations in the distribution of cars ; for instance, during one period of five hundred and sixty-four days, as was proven in court, they delivered to the Pittsburg Coal Company, 2,371 empty cars to be loaded with coal, although such company had sale for, and capacity to produce and load, during the same period, more than 15,000 cars. During the same time this railway company delivered to the Rogers Coal Company, in which the railway company and C. W. Rogers, its vice-president and general manager, were interested, no less than 15,483 coal cars, while 456 were delivered to individual shippers. In other words, the coal company owned in large part by the railway and its officials was given eighty-two per cent of all the facilities to get coal to market, although the other shippers had much greater combined capacity than had the Rogers Coal Company.

"During the last four months of the period named, and when the Pittsburg Coal Company had the plant, force, and capacity to load thirty cars per day, they received an average of one and a fourth cars per day, resulting, as was intended, in the utter ruin of a prosperous business and the involuntary sale of the property, while the railway coal company, the railway officials, and the accommodating friends who operated the Rogers Coal Company, made vast sums of money ; and when all the other shippers had thus been driven off the line the price of coal was advanced to the consumer.

"On another railway, traversing the same coal-field, the railway or its officials became interested in the Keith and Perry Coal Company—the largest coal company

doing business on the line—and here the plan seems to
have been in addition to the manipulation of rates, to
starve other mine operators out, and force them to sell
their coal to the Keith and Perry Company, by failing to
furnish the needed cars to those who did not sell their
coal to the Keith and Perry Company at a very low
price.

"When the Keith and Perry Company had a great
demand for coal, such parties as sold the product of their
mines to that company were furnished with cars, but for
the other operators cars were not to be had, such cars as
were brought to the field being assigned to such parties as
were loading to the Keith and Perry Company, because
that company furnished the coal consumed by the locomotives of the railway.

"One operator. after being for years forced in this way
to sell his product to the Keith and Perry Company, or
see his several plants stand idle, has, in recent months,
been obliged to build some seven miles of railway in
order to reach four different roads, and thus have a fight-
ing chance for cars, although all these railways were
provided with coal mines owned by the corporations or
their officials.

"In Arkansas, Jay Gould, or his railway company,
own coal mines, and the coal is transported to the
neighboring town at low rates, and there is an ample
supply of cars for such mines ; but the owners of an
adjoining mine are forced to haul their coal some eighteen
miles to the same town in wagons, as the rates charged
them over Mr. Gould's railway are so high as to absorb
the value of the coal at destination.

"The Colorado Coal and Iron Company produce all the
anthracite coal sold in Colorado. It is mined at Crested
Butte, which is 150 miles nearer Leadville than Denver,
yet this coal is sold in Leadville for $9.00 to the individual
consumer, while the same coal is hauled 150 miles farther,
and sold to the individual consumer for an advance of
but twenty-five cents per ton over the Leadville price.

23. *Railroad companies also secure timber lands, erect saw mills and do a large lumber business.* And also unite with some of the " protected " lumber producers in the exaction of exorbitant prices for lumber.

24. *They employ agents or become interested with men engaged in business and become shippers over their own lines,* in this way handling grain, livestock or other commodities. This forms a wide field for their operations, especially for unscrupulous railway managers, who, by giving their agents especial advantages in lower rates or rebates, and a better supply of cars, make their road a hard one for competing shippers to use and enable them to use the railroad power to enrich themselves.

" The only answer thus far made by the apologists for these practices has been to denounce those who opposed them as 'communists' or 'socialists.' So bare of facts and so hard pushed for arguments favorable to their case are they, that Messrs. Vanderbilt and Jewett must fain adopt this policy, and conjure up the phantom of socialism to shield their practices ! In their joint letter to the Hepburn Committee they suggest that the staid and conservative merchants of the New York Chamber of Commerce are fast tending in that direction, their words being : —

" The growth of a disregard of property in this country is very marked, and railroad corporations offer favorable forms of attack. The encouragement by such a body as the Chamber of Commerce to such ideas will not stop at railroad corporations, but will reach all kinds of associated capital, and will not stop before it reaches all property. This growing tendency to socialistic principles is one of the dangerous signs of the times, and, if not checked, will produce scenes of disaster that would appall the country.

"Some months after this, when the Legislative committee had pronounced the principal charges made by the Chamber of Commerce ' fully proven,' the committee of that body having the matter in charge alluded to this subject, in their report to the Chamber, as follows : —

" ' Your committee beg that the members of the Chamber of Commerce, will carefully compare these utterances of Messrs. Vanderbilt and Jewett with the findings of the Legislative committee.   The assertion that the action of this Chamber tends to the encouragement of socialistic or communistic principles, is on a parity with much of the other reasoning of the presidents of the great trunk lines.   They seem to be entirely oblivious of the fact that it is their disregard of public rights, and not the efforts which this Chamber has made to compel their observation, which is chiefly responsible for the growth of communistic sentiment in this state.   If railroads were not public highways, upon which all shippers, as well as passengers, are entitled to equal rights ; *if the discovery of steam, and its application to the purposes of transportation, and all its attendant benefits, could be esteemed alone the private property of these gentlemen, then the argument of Messrs. Vanderbilt and Jewett might be considered valid, and the efforts of our committee seditious, socialistic, and worthy of condemnation.*

"It is hardly necessary to say that your committee have no sympathy with socialists or communists who want something for nothing ; this class of persons might perhaps find fault with your committee for being capitalists ; but, on the other hand, we can not uphold a system of operating public highways · which is honey-combed with abuses, and which is controlled absolutely by a few individuals who tax production and commerce at will, and who practically dictate what reward the producer, manufacturer, and merchant shall receive for his labor." (From article of Mr. Thurber in *Scribner* of December, 1880.)

The big railway corporation is many sided.   It is

always reaching out for other fields from which to gather a harvest. Its mills are big and it exacts heavy tolls. It is insatiable. It has a powerful grasp and wonderful capacity for the absorption of wealth.

It is difficult to estimate the annual loss to the nation and the people from the present railway management. We know that there is a large number of railway millionaires with wealth ranging from $5,000,000 to $100-000,000, and that this wealth has been mostly accumulated in the past twenty to thirty years, and it is still rapidly increasing. We know that there is a vast amount annually wasted by present methods. Mr. Davis estimates the amount that could be saved under national ownership by correcting and simplifying the management to be about $160,000,000 a year. But this takes into account only the saving of present expense which would be unnecessary under the national ownership. It does not include the loss to the people from discriminations, exorbitant charges, profits of construction and over-capitalizing, exactions on account of coal and lumber and shipping, and other sources of profit to the railway managers or loss and waste to the people.

We may fairly assume that the amount of wealth annually lost to the people, and which either goes to the railway capitalists and railway men, or to loss and waste, is about $500-000,000 and perhaps much more.

CHAPTER XXIII.

MR. C. P. HUNTINGTON ON RAILWAY CONSOLIDATION

Mr. C. P. Huntington, President of the Union Pacific Railway Company, in his article entitled "A plea for Railway Consolidation," in the *North American Review* for September, 1891, has given such excellent arguments for national ownership of the railways that I make an extended extract from it. Do not understand that he advocates national ownership, but his argument fits our case admirably. He says : (The italics are the author's.)

" What possible remedy is there for such a state of things except joint ownership ? As a simple business proposition it seems to me unanswerable, for, by its application, it can be readily seen that *much of the expense of maintaining separate organization and separate offices will be cut off and a great multitude of agents and agencies will be dispensed with.* On the side of the people quite as much good will be the outcome. The complaint of charging more for a short than a long haul, which comes from the shipper located between instead of at the important centers, will cease to be heard, *because the pernicious system of giving rebates and commissions,* or whatever they may be called, *that cost the road so much money* and really do their patrons as a whole, so much harm, *will no longer be practised,* the excuse or necessity therefor no longer existing.

" While the uniting of small roads has been productive of great benefits to the owners and to the public who use them, yet *I am satisfied that the best results will not be*

149

reached until substantially all the transportation business of this country is done by one company. The accomplishment of this would reduce the cost of transportation to the minimum which would admit of the lowest possible rates to shippers and passengers." (That is correct, but we, the people, must see that the whole transportation question is put under a control which will not only "*admit* of the lowest possible rates, but which will *secure* and *insure* them to us and to our posterity. Author.) "There would be no longer any necessity of charging more for a short than a long haul, except where water competition existed as the crossing of railroads at various points would have no further effect upon the rate schedules.

"The raising of rates at non-competing points is one of the things done by railroads which it is hard to explain to the satisfaction of those who buy transportation ; but it will continue to be done as long as railroads are controlled by scattered interests, and *neither arguments nor laws will entirely prevent it.* If, on the contrary, all the railroads of the country were held in joint ownership, they *would need much less rolling stock* than is now required, as the great staple crops of the country are moved at different seasons of the year, and cars and locomotives could be transferred from one section to another as needed, thus saving a large amount of capital which otherwise, for a considerable portion of the year, would be idle.

"There is *another feature of this question,* that is perhaps hardly taken into account in the public mind, because its bearing upon it appears, at first glance, to be remote ; but we are dealing with a problem of the future, and the time is coming when its close relation to it will be appreciated. The existence of an undoubted security for institutions and for the great mass of conservative investors of limited means, who demand above all other qualifications a security that shall be safe, and who rely upon their investments for the incomes which are to support themselves and their families, is soon to become a necessity in America. Our government bonds are constantly being called in and cancelled, whilst the surplus capital of the country is continually increasing. Unless a stable and safe security for the multitude is forthcoming, it does not need the astuteness of a financier to comprehend the possible situation of the future when the investor who seeks an assured income from his savings will have to place his reliance upon the wisdom of his own selection among a list of many hundreds of railway stocks and bonds, *subject to all the serious fluctuations that follow in the wake of selfish competition and inefficient management.*

" The writer has never regarded the existence of a large national debt as an evil in a prosperous and growing country like the United States, whose obligations do not affect the credit of the government and are not significant of any financial embarassment ; but our people have decided otherwise, perhaps not unwisely ; nevertheless there must be a substitute for the people to invest their savings in a security that shall possess the confidence of the entire public. What shall it be ? It seems to the writer that nothing will be safer than shares or bonds of the united railroads of this country, and few, if any, other securities will be so easy to negotiate or raise money on. If this is true, why should not a very large number of the people who use these roads invest their money in such an organization, and thus become, to a large extent, the owners and controllers of the railroads that they use? " (The people would have very little to say about the *control* with the controlling interest in the hands of the present managers, but, with the control in the government their voice would be the end of the law. The above argument for the necessity of a safe security in which the people may invest their savings is an additional argument for national ownership, for no security is safer than United States bonds. Author.)

" All are interested in having the enormous tonnage of

food gathered and distributed at the lowest possible cost. It can not be done by little fragmentary companies, for they cannot practice the economies of wealth, as their poor road-beds, crippled rolling stock, and lean management will testify.   What is wanted is not more than two or three—and one would be better—great carrying companies, with their steel tracks and road-beds as nearly perfect as they can be, with all their machinery of the best quality, with their capacious warehouses at intermediate points and their almost unlimited terminal facilities.   (Note that about the big warehouses. *The big combine would do the entire shipping business of the country.* It would handle by its own agents every product of field, forest, mill and mine. Author.)   With the best talent in the country to manage and control such an organization *many millions could be saved to those who use the railroads of this country, and millions also to those who own them over what is now being received by the fragmentary, badly equipped and inefficiently managed roads that, with but few exceptions, now exist.*

"To be sure there are demagogues who cry ' Monopoly !' and assert that the great corporations are about to override the liberties of the people ; but solicitude for the people is not the real reason of their outcry.   It is because they hope to climb upon the noise they make into higher places, and into seats that they are not worthy of and have not the ability to fill."

CHAPTER XXIV

THE TELEGRAPH

The people of the United States are much behind those of most other countries in allowing the great railway highways to be controlled by private corporations, but *we are far behind the age* in still leaving the telegraph, which is properly a part of the mail service, in the control of a greedy monopoly. *The United States is the only enlightened nation of any importance on the Globe in which the telegraph is not under government control.*

The charge for telegraphic service in the United States is so exorbitant that people of moderate means usually do not resort to its use except in cases of great emergency ; and the cost of press dispatches is so heavy that only leading city dailies can afford to pay for them. The telegraph service costs much more here than in other countries, and we do not reap the benefit from this great means of diffusing knowledge throughout the country that we should do. The telegraph should go wherever the mails go, and the price of a telegram should be so low that the humblest citizen might avail himself of its advantages. And the cost of press dispatches should be brought within the reach of the thousands of smaller dailies in country towns which now can not afford them. Indeed the very existence of a daily press often depends upon its ability to obtain press dispatches, and if these were furnished at as low prices as they are in most other countries, the price of daily papers could be brought within the reach of thousands who now cannot afford to take them.

The people of the United States should no longer permit this great institution for the transmission of intelligence and the diffusion of knowledge, to be used as a means for diverting a stream of wealth from the people's necessities to a millionaire's pocket, or to fall so far short of being to the fullest extent a means for disseminating knowledge among the common people.

The mail service is extended to the remotest points in the nation, and with the telegraph under government management, it would be extended to most points where mail is now delivered.

In England the telegraph has been owned and managed by the government for over twenty years. The telegraph service is a part of the mail service. The service has been largely extended, the cost of messages much reduced, and the number increased about one thousand per cent. Mr. W. H. Preece, F. R. S., Vice-President of the Society of Arts of London, read a paper before the Society in May, 1887, entitled "Fifty Years Progress in Telegraphy," in which he speaks of the results of government ownership of the telegraph lines in the United Kingdom as follows : —

"One of the great objections raised against the absorption of the telegraph by the state was the difficulty which the government would have in transmitting news. In no country is there now such a complete system of telegraphy for news purposes as there is in the United Kingdom. Whenever any great political event arises, such as the delivery of a great speech, all the important towns throughout the kingdom receive simultaneously a *verbatim* report of the speech. There is not a town in the country where a daily paper is printed which is not placed after 6 P. M., in direct communication with London and where there is not deposited on every subscriber's breakfast table a nearly *verbatim* report of the previous night's debate in Parliament.

"It is amusing after this length of time, to read the arguments that were adduced against the absorption of the telegraphs by the state. Every reason has been proved wrong, every prophecy has remained unfulfilled. I can say this with a good grace for I was one of the prophets.

" The advantages of a state controlled telegraph system have been amply shown. There has been established a cheaper, more widely extended, and more expeditious system of telegraphy ; the wires have been erected in districts that private companies could not reach ; the cost of telegrams has been reduced, not only in their transmission but in their delivery ; the number of offices opened has been trebled ; a provincial and an evening press have been virtually created."

The charge for the transmission of a telegram between any two points in the United Kingdom is twelve cents for the first twelve words and one cent for each additional word, including the address and signature, and the average charge for press messages is about five cents for each one hundred words. Any one familiar with the charges for messages and press dispatches in this country will note the wide difference in cost between the two countries.

I have quoted from the able article of Mr. Shelby M. Cullom in the *Forum* for February, 1888, entitled "The Goverment and the Telegraph," as authority for some of the statements given in regard to the success of national owned telegraphs in the United Kingdom, including the extract from the address of Mr. Preece.

CHAPTER XXV

OBJECTIONS TO NATIONAL OWNERSHIP OF RAIL-WAY AND TELEGRAPH LINES CONSIDERED

1. *That it would give wide room for political power and for corruption and peculation.* This is the most common objection. It has already been answered in the article on civil service reform.

We have no such difficulty with the naval or military service, the treasury, mint, or life saving service, very little in the mail service, and we have very little any where except as the legitimate and inevitable result of the abominable spoils system. On the other hand the present unscrupulous railroad management is one of the most corrupting influences on our modern politics, which, if removed, would carry with it one of the chief sources of corruption.

The short answer to this objection and to those which grow out of it, is that the men who inaugurate national ownership of railroads in this country should at the same time and with the same spirit put a final end to the disgraceful spoils system in the management of our national affairs, and should see to it that in fact, as well as in name, "a public office" shall be "a public trust," and that all our public servants be selected for the one purpose of rightly serving the people.

2. *That it would create a heavy and burdensome debt, and that the people would have to be taxed to pay it.* This is an

objection and the only real one. But it is not by any
means as serious as it at first appears. It is not an
obstacle, and not a very serious difficulty.

It would not be necessary for the nation to acquire
all of the roads at once, or to acquire any which
are not needed for the public service. The present
bond and shareholders would readily take government bonds in lieu of their present holdings. United
States bonds are better securities than railway bonds or
shares. In buying, the nation should pay for actual
values only—should buy railways and not water. There
is no reason why the people should pay any more than
actual values, what it would cost to duplicate the property,
less wear and tear. The people would owe the railway
companies nothing for "good will " or established business. Franchises and privileges granted would cover all
that.

The civil war, including the pension debt, cost the
nation a sum untold—probably over $10,000,000,000.
We are now paying about $140,000,000 annually for pen-
sions, and the pension debt, under present laws, is now
something like $3,000,000,000. Yet the bulk of this
immense war debt has been actually paid by the
people.

The railroads would cost the nation to buy or condemn
about $5,000,000,000, or possibly $6,000,000,000. But
they need not and would not cost a single citizen a single
dollar, because *the railroads would be a source of profit and
not of loss. They would pay for themselves.*

Our war debt represented a loss. There was nothing
to show as an offset (except a united country.) It had
to be paid by the toil of the people. But the debt

incurred by the nation in buying the railways will represent an investment, and a *paying investment*. The bonds issued in the purchase of the roads need not, necessarily, be paid by the people. The roads will stand as an offset to the bonds, and will always be worth what they cost. The productive value of the roads will be constantly increasing as population and wealth increase, and the operating expenses will proportionately decrease, as road beds, rolling stock, motive power and appliances are improved.

It would be a paying investment in a triple sense, first in the increased comfort, security and satisfaction, and decreased cost to the people ; second by paying all cost of operating expenses and fixed charges, including interest on the bonds and a moderate sinking fund for the payment of the bonds if thought best ; and third (and on this point I shall have more to say in another place) should be in a measure a source of revenue to the government, for how could we more easily secure a revenue or with less burden to ourselves?

A debt which represents a paying investment in productive property, especially where it is a source of revenue besides paying for care of the property, for cost of doing the business and interest on the investment, and where ample time is allowed for final payment, is not a burden either to an individual or a nation.

Besides, the people, not bankers and capitalists only. but those who have smaller savings and need a safe investment—need a security that can be relied on, and the nation should increase rather than decrease its bonded debt, provided the debt is represented by its value in productive property.

If we grant the force of this objection, we would still insist that the burden of such a debt would be small compared with the burden of the present railway system.

3. *That it would be another step toward a centralized, paternal and tyrannical government.*

This objection corresponds to a theory of government which has been expounded if not originated by a school of political economists of the Herbert Spencer type. Their contention is, that the government should protect each citizen in his or her equal rights against any encroachments from other citizens, and that in properly doing this the whole duty and prerogative of the government ends so far as individuals are concerned ; that when the government undertakes to establish and maintain schools, alms-houses and asylums ; a life-saving service, a weather signal service, a health service ; to build roads, bridges, canals, breakwaters, lighthouses, dykes, water works ; to carry mails and establish banks of exchange, it goes beyond its legitimate powers, and is paternal, dictatorial and tyrannical.

A plain statement of this theory and what it would lead to is its sufficient refutation in this day and age. And yet we have able and scholarly men who advocate such a theory. It is individualism run mad. It would lead to almost no government at all. It means to turn back the wheels of progress for a thousand years and leave us in a state of barbarism.

4. *That it is in the line of socialism and nationalism, and is wild, impractical and visionary.*

It would seem that the " paternal " and the " socialistic " objections were contradictory and would answer each

other.   Those who object to what they term socialism in
managing state affairs appear to be satisfied with what
is already being done in that direction.   The things that
we have undertaken to do as a whole people by the government have proven beneficial.   National co-operation
in managing some of our business affairs has been to
our advantage.   The state makes a success of the schools,
the nation of the mail service, and so on.   But, if we do
this it would be socialism, and if we do that it would be
nationalism, and those would be very bad things to
introduce I   Such alarms have been sounded without
showing wherein the danger lies, without pointing out
what might or might not properly be done by the nation,
or what would and what would not be conservative
business methods.

We must differentiate.   We must show what we should
do, and what we should not do as a nation.   We need to
draw the line between the legitimate powers and prerogatives of government on the one hand, and the unwise,
and unsafe socialistic tendencies and practices on the
other.   And we need to do this, not only in view of what
we may do, but of what we are already doing.   For we
have now in some instances gone beyond the bounds of
conservative business methods, have superseded any
legitimate powers of government, and have yielded to a
tendency toward unwise socialism.

CHAPTER XXVI

THE TRUE PROVINCE OF GOVERNMENT, DUTY OF THE STATE, CONSERVATIVE METHODS AND UNSAFE TENDENCIES.

The powers and duties of government are: To protect and care for the citizen in life, liberty, property and happiness ; to protect him from thefts, slander, assault, nuisance, annoyance, contagion, and from temptations of the saloon, lottery, gaming table and other snares; to establish schools, asylums, hospitals, reformatories, pesthouses, quarantines ; to maintain highways, harbors, mail service, to provide a currency, and to carry on any other public business or enterprise which will promote the best interests of the people and strengthen the state, and which the people can not as well, as safely, as economically, as efficiently do for themselves.

It is the duty of the state to do these things, to the end that the health, the morals, the intelligence, the safety, the sobriety, the good order, the comfort, the usefulness and happiness of the people shall be conserved.

The state, in carrying on its business and affairs, should be guided by the same principles of sound policy and substantial business methods which should control the individual in like circumstances. When the state, in the conduct of any beneficent institution, as the public schools, goes beyond the required object for which the institution was founded, it exceeds its legitimate province and is unwise. When, in the management of any business, as the mail service, the nation fails to conduct the business on a strictly business basis, it passes the line of conservative government, and, to that extent, is unsafe. That we have passed the line in some instances is a fact to which our attention should be directed, to the end that we should retrace our steps where we have gone˙ too far, and should guard against such tendencies in the future.

The state maintains public schools in order to give the young such training as will make them moral, patriotic, intelligent and useful citizens. Referring to a city high school curriculum, we find that over one-half the time of the four years' course is taken up with higher mathematics and foreign languages. Without questioning the advantage or utility of such studies to certain professions, and conceding the prerogative of the state to fit young men and women for special vocations in life, it is safe to say that these studies are not necessary or especially useful or desirable to the ordinary student, and not requisite to fit the boy for intelligent and useful citizenship or to become a competent legislator, and that the state, in taxing all the people in order to teach studies which can never be applied, supersedes its legitimate powers, and is in that line unwise and socialistic.

Studies which are not useful in themselves and only applicable as a means of acquiring knowledge, should not be taught except as a preparation for other studies. Nor should the time of the student be so curtailed while it is far too limited in which to acquire a satisfactory knowledge of the many branches which should be taught in the schools.

To the student who is being fitted for a vocation—as engineering or pedagogy—requiring special mathematic or linguistic attainment, such branches become a necessary part of the special course. But, in the general course of study, only branches which have some application in the course or in after life, should be taught. (We have in this, however, an instance of moss-back conservatism, which has led to extreme socialism.)

The mail service is now conducted at a loss to the department. There have been times when it was on a paying basis, that is, not counting any fixed charges, such as interest on cost of buildings, etc., owned by the government. Every business enterprise of an individual or nation should stand on its own footing. Those who send letters and papers through the mails should pay for the sending. It is wrong in principle for the nation in a business matter to tax all the people for the benefit of a part. And it is unsafe for the nation to do any business at a loss. And yet we are liable to hear some statesman (?) propose a reduction of postal rates and a still greater loss to the nation. With the nation owning the railways we could readily put the mail service on a paying basis at present rates, as the deficit is not large. The charges for mail service should be close to cost in order to encourage the dissemination of intelligence, but there should be no deficit. Let us retrace our steps and hereafter keep on the solid road.

It is proper and just that those who have served the nation in the army or navy. in the life saving or other service, and who have suffered in health or usefulness thereby should be suitably compensated by the nation for their loss. But it is not wise or just that *all* who

serve the state in such capacity should be made pen-
sioners of the state, regardless of needs, or time, or service, or loss. I speak as a veteran soldier of the civil war
and from what I deem patriotic motives toward my old
comrades and to all the people alike, in saying that, in
my judgment, we have gone fully far enough in this line,
and that for the government to grant a service pension
to all old soldiers, simply because they served in the
army or navy would be unwise and unjust. It would be
a heavy tax and an unnecessary one upon the people, and
would be a bad precedent. There is no good reason why a
citizen simply because he has served in the army, should
become a pensioner and a burden upon the nation, while
he is well able to take care of himself. All tendencies in
this direction are toward a socialism which is not wise,
or just, or prudent. To grant a life pension to a man
who is ailing because he served ninety days in the home
guards is not wise. To grant a life pension to all who
served in the army, including those of such short term
service, would be folly. And yet we have statesmen (?)
who advocate such a measure, and appeal to the nation
" to do justice to the old soldiers." No patriotic soldier
will ask of the nation any such " justice."

When the nation owns the railways, we may expect to
hear a clamor from a class or party to give us " transportation at cost," and with a tendency to make it less
than cost. And we will surely have demagogues who
will advocate the lowest possible rates, and that the government can pay the deficit. Such a policy would be in
a high degree unbusiness-like, and would tend to financial
loss, discredit and disaster. *A socialism which demands
something for nothing, which asks to be taken in and cared*

*for without money and without price, which wants some
one else to do the work and some one else to " pay the piper,"*
is of the kind that we should avoid. Labor must be
paid. Capital must be paid. When we as a nation employ labor and capital we should pay just the same as
individuals would in like circumstances, and we should
require every member of the company, who is able, to
pay his part.

The people of Australia made the mistake of making
railway rates so low that the roads were operated at a loss.
Of course the people got a large benefit from the low
rates. They started out with the idea of getting " transportation at cost," and as a result got it at less than
cost.

The receipts and expenditures of any business, change
with the times and seasons. The only safe way to do
any business, is to do it on a margin which will cover all
possible expense and loss. Hundreds of grange and
co-operative stores in this country went to the wall,
because the people undertook to get their goods at cost,
that is without making a profit, and as a result, though
for a while they got their goods at less than cost, the
prices not covering the expense of handling, the stores
necessarily became bankrupt.

The people of Australia saw their mistake and have
sturdily set themselves to rectify it. They have lost
nothing so far, but they started in a way to lose everything, and they do not propose to follow that road any
longer. Let us profit by their example.

*In the principle of government ownership and manage-
ment* of our railway and other great monopolies, lies the
remedy for much of the privation among our laboring

masses.   This principle should be the "cloud by day and
the fire by night" to lead us out of the wilderness of
monopoly with which we are environed. *It is the principle that the people themselves,* by their chosen servants,
should carry on their own business, and do it for their own
profit and benefit, and that the conduct and management
of their most important and most profitable business
affairs *should not be* any longer *farmed out*—placed in the
hands of private corporations, to use these opportunities
for their own enrichment and aggrandizement.

And the reasons and principles which will lead us to
undertake the conduct of all our means of transportation
and communication will also ultimately lead us to undertake government management of many of our financial,
industrial and commercial monopolies, as well.

CHAPTER XXVII

*THE CURRENCY. EVILS OF OUR FINANCIAL
SYSTEM. COIN AND PAPER MONEY. THE
NATIONAL BANKS.*

The question of money does not demand a leading
place in a consideration of causes and remedies of poverty.   It does not merit the almost exclusive attention
that is given it as a political question by some of the
American people.   The financial question is a somewhat
complicated one, and no other political question, except
that of tariff, is so beclouded in the minds of many of

our people.   In relation to no other national question are
so many fallacious ideas advanced, or so many mischiev-
ous measures advocated.   There are several plans for
" financial relief " proposed, which, if adopted, would
inevitably tend to increase rather than diminish the
burdens of the laboring classes.

It is true that there are serious evils and defects in our
present financial system, and that several reforms are
justly demanded.   There have been financial measures
adopted by our government which were unjust—favoring
the monied class and burdensome to the masses of the
people, and there are several reforms which should be
inaugurated which would be a relief and a benefit to the
people.   While the evils of our present financial system
have been by some overrated, still there is much room for
reform.

The government should furnish and maintain a sufficient and stable currency, and this should be done without
the intervention of private corporations ; it should furnish
to the people a safe depository for their money, and should
pay interest upon their deposits ; it should loan money
to the people in such manner as the banks now do, and
should reduce interest charges.   The nation should be
the chief banker ; should control and regulate the money
supply ; should retain for the whole people the profits
accruing from the money business.   The government
should no longer give special privileges and immunities to a banking class ; should no longer subsidize national banks ; should cease to make donations
to banks by furnishing banking capital in the way
of deposits without security or interest ; should not
pay bounty and tribute to the money power.   And the

people should no longer be obliged to pay tribute to this power and be subject to its exactions. *The national banks should go.*

Money is primarily coin, a precious metal or other highly valuable commodity, stamped by public authority for use as a standard measure of values and a convenient medium of exchange and means of storing wealth. The best money is that which may be used in any civilized country with little or no discount from its face value. In all ages, gold and silver have been the precious metals most used as money by civilized nations. Nickel, copper, brass, spelter, ivory, beads, etc., are also used as money, secondary to gold and silver or by uncivilized people.

Gold is the standard of value in nearly all civilized nations, because it fluctuates in value less than other metals and is more convenient for use in all large transactions. Gold has had a recognized intrinsic value in all ages and among all civilized peoples, more fixed, more unchangeable than that of any other material thing, and its value as a standard measure of values has never been overrated. Silver had, during long periods of time, a value nearly as fixed as that of gold, but during the last four decades it has been depreciating in value, and can no longer be counted upon as a standard of money equal to gold. This depreciation has been brought about, not by edicts or decrees of nations, but by the fact of a production of silver beyond the demand for it, either for money or art uses, to an extent which could but act to reduce its relative value.

It has not been found practicable to use two metals as standards of value. Any fluctuation in the value of either metal disturbs the relative value, and parity cannot be maintained. Attempts by the United States or by any other nation to use both gold and silver as standard money have always resulted in one or other being withdrawn from circulation, the most valuable being hoarded or sold. Silver is therefore used by our own and by most other nations as a " subsidiary " or tributary coin to gold, and made a legal tender for a small fixed sum. Gold is almost universally used for coin payments of five dollars and over, and silver, nickel and copper for smaller amounts.

Secondarily, we have *paper money*, any " promise to pay " which may be used instead of coin, its value depending wholly upon the ability and readiness to pay of the power which issues it, and upon the confidence which people have in that ability and integrity. A plain bank check is " good as gold " with those who have confidence in the ability and integrity of the maker, otherwise it must be " certified " by an official of the bank on which it is drawn in order to be readily received. United States notes and national bank notes are " as good as the gold " while the people have confidence in the ability and integrity of the nation to pay them in gold. But we have had such unhappy and disastrous experiences with depreciated bank notes and with depreciated United States notes as well—with the promises and obligations of individuals and of states and nations—that we know that promises to pay are not quite as good as the pay. It is something like the case of the baker we read of who held out the loaf through his window with one hand while he took the coin in the other. The promise may be good in a week or a month ; it may be good in ten years or in twenty years, and it may not be.

The future is unknown. No man or company of men can foresee the results of the many forces acting to-day, and of the many new forces which may be in the coming years. We should therefore make only such promises as we may reasonably hope to fulfill.

United States notes are now practically as good as gold and will probably continue to be so. But their value *depends* upon the wisdom of the nation in conducting its financial affairs. While wise counsels obtain, our paper will retain its present value, but should unwise and unsafe counsels prevail, our paper money would certainly become depreciated. With confidence in the good business sense of a large majority of the American people, we do not apprehend any serious danger of the latter result.

The evils of our National bank system. It is an error and a wrong that we subsidize the national banks. While this is true, it is also true that our government now offers less inducement than formerly for the organization of national banks. The crying evil of this system as a means of subsidizing the monied class is largely a thing of the past. When a national bank could buy six per cent bonds, draw the interest on them, and also receive from the government ninety per cent of bank notes on the amount of bonds purchased, and loan this amount at ten to fifteen per cent, at the same time securing the name, the prestige and the supervision of the national government for the one per cent, tax paid, that was a crying evil and an unwarranted favor and bounty given to the banking class. But now, any new national banks, or those old ones wishing to extend their issue after the bonds they now hold are called in, must buy government two per cent bonds, so that there is but small profit to a

bank in an issue of currency on those terms.   Still it is
an evil and should be abated.

The capital of banks consists of their capital stock,
accrued profits, issue of notes, and money of depositors,
and their income is derived mostly from loans.   Usually
the larger part of their capital is the money of depositors,
upon which, as a rule, they pay no interest, and from
which they make most of their profits.   The people furnish this money to the banks without remuneration,
and pay the banks large sums in the aggregate for
interest charges upon loans.   The banks obtain this money
without cost and without giving security, and they loan
it at high rates of interest and upon good security, and
*herein lies the principal cost and loss to the people from our
present banking system, national and state.*

The question of banking which is of first importance
to the American people, is that *the people should themselves
have the profits accruing to the banking business;* the nation
should be the banker and the whole people should receive
the benefit.   *This is the chief and almost the only question
which should demand our attention in regard to this question of financial reform.*   The people, by their national
representatives, should do their own banking business
and receive all the benefits to be derived from it, instead
of "farming it out" to money corporations ; subsidizing
them, and allowing them to lay a heavy burden of tax
upon us by exorbitant interest charges.   Let us in this
matter do our own business, and not put ourselves in a
position to be subject to the exaction of a set of men
whom we allow to control our financial interests and to
a considerable extent our commercial interests, as well.
Let us in this matter "keep shop" for ourselves.

The demand that the government shall issue money to the people without the intervention of banks, and without profit to any corporation, is a just demand. No more national banks should be chartered, no more bank issues extended, and as fast as the bank notes are called in and cancelled, treasury notes should be issued to take their place. The government now has large sums of money deposited with certain national banks without security and without interest. This practice should cease.

CHAPTER XXVIII

POSTAL SAVINGS BANKS. IMPROVEMENTS IN POSTAL EXCHANGE

The principal reform needed in our financial system is the inauguration of banks of deposit in connection with the postoffice department or otherwise, in order that the government may deal directly with the people in money matters. The postal savings bank would afford the credit of the nation as security for the safety of deposits, and would furnish bank facilities in localities where a private bank would not be supported. Our present banks, national and state, do not always furnish a safe depository. We need national banks which furnish to depositors the security of the nation, and the postal savings banks would have this advantage over all others.

The money so deposited should be loaned to the people

on the security of bonds, stocks, mortgages, warehouse receipts, standing crops or other convertible property as collateral to personal security, or on personal security alone, *always provided that the security be ample*—such as would be satisfactory with any other reputable bank.

The government bank should do business in such a manner as not to become liable in a business transaction of having to make any donations to individuals. For the government, in a benevolent way, to care for the sick or infirm is laudable, but it should not undertake to provide for those who are able to care for themselves.

But money should not be loaned by these banks upon land security except upon mortgages used as a secondary security, and in such manner as not to call for the sale of the land, but of the mortgage, to secure payment of the loan. Nor should the money be loaned upon long time, usually not longer than three to six months.

The legitimate province of banking is to furnish a safe depository for the savings of the people, to pay interest on deposits, and to loan money to those who need it to assist them temporarily in carrying on their business, at certain times or seasons when they require additional capital; it is *not to furnish a capital* with which to do a business or to buy land.

The government should probably pay from two to four per cent interest to depositors, and loan the money at from four to six per cent, in either case depending upon locality, demand, amount and time. The rates must necessarily correspond to some extent with those prevailing in the localities. The government should not undertake any sudden or extreme bull or bear movement in the money market or in any other line of business.

There is no reason why officials of the postoffice. in
localities where sufficient business might be done to
afford the employment of skilled men. should not carry
on a legitimate and safe banking business for the people.
Such offices are now usually kept by men who are
thoroughly competent and reliable. Another advantage
of the national savings bank system would be, that
money which accumulates as a surplus in some localities
at certain seasons, could be loaned in other localities,
where for the time, the needs of business, as in harvesting,
or handling stock or crops, made a stronger demand for
money. Thus, money need not be lying idle in one state
or locality while much needed in another.

Improvements in Postal Exchange. Our present system
of postal exchange by postoffice order is unnecessarily
complicated, expensive and cumbersome, and is insufficient. It should be simplified, cheapened and extended.
Small sums (perhaps up to five dollars) might be sent
readily by a postal card device, at a nominal price of two to
three cents, the security of the remittance depending
upon the identification of the payee. Such a device
would be a great convenience and saving to those sending
small sums, as for paying subscriptions to newspapers
and magazines, purchase of books, etc., and would greatly
facilitate the circulation of periodicals. and be a pronounced means for the diffusion of intelligence among
the people. For larger sums postal drafts should be
used.

CHAPTER XXIX

MONEY MONOPOLY? IS THERE A GREAT SCARCITY
OF MONEY? DO WE NEED FIFTY DOLLARS PER
CAPITA? MONEY SUPPLY OF DIFFERENT
NATIONS. SCARCITY OF MONEY NOT THE CAUSE
OF THE FARMER'S DEPRESSION

It is not strange that there should be a prevailing idea
that much of the depression among the industrial classes
is caused by a scarcity of money, by a monopoly of money
by the wealthy classes, and by legislation in the interest of
bankers and capitalists. Many of us greatly need more
money, or at least more wealth, and if we had plenty of
money we could get everything we need, and it seems a
logical conclusion that there must be a great scarcity of
money and that this is a chief cause of financial depression.
We have been often told that there has been a great contraction of the currency, that there is not nearly enough
money in circulation to do the business of the country on
a cash basis, and that the bankers and brokers have a
monopoly of money, and try to keep it scarce in order to
get a good price for it. And we are told that to remedy
these evils we should have forty or fifty or one hundred
dollars per capita in circulation in order to facilitate the
transaction of the business of the country and make
times good ; that the volume of the currency should be
increased by the issue of treasury notes and by the " free
and unlimited coinage of silver," and that this money

175

should be loaned to the people on the security of land or
of non-perishable farm products, until the demand was
supplied and "good times" restored. ·

Is there a great scarcity of money?   Has any man wheat
or cattle, corn or cotton, or other articles for which there is
a demand, which he cannot sell for what they are worth
in general markets, considering cost of transport and
other charges and expense under our present methods
of business and which we can account for aside from any
scarcity of money?   Has a man labor to sell for which
there is a demand, for which he may not receive pay in
coin?   Is there a locality in the Union—in Massachusetts,
Ohio, Iowa or other state, where there is not enough money,
as a rule, to do the legitimate business of the community?
At times, in some localities there may be a scarcity, but,
as a rule, in any city or in the country at large there is
not.

When there is a scarcity of money in any locality it is
because the "balance of trade" is against it, the people
of the locality failing to have enough commodities for
sale to pay for articles needed for consumption.

In Pasadena during boom times we had a large supply
of town lots for sale for which there was a strong demand
at high prices, and we had plenty of money, but, after
the boom, there being no demand for our lots, and as we
had neglected our other industries, we had few products
to sell and money became scarce.   In Denver, Spokane,
and many other places such conditions have prevailed.
But, in Southern California the ranch man who has a
good crop of oranges or alfalfa or walnuts or other salable
products, has no difficulty in exchanging them for coin.
And the same is true of the Mississippi cotton planter,

the Illinois corn grower, or any other successful producer. An Iowa farmer says that in his locality there is an abundance of money in the banks, and that farms and farm products sell readily for cash.

A failure of crops causes a scarcity of money among the farmers, and this reacts upon the towns. But all this depends upon lack of wealth or production in a locality and not upon lack of money in the country at large. *Poverty and hard times depend mainly, not upon lack of wealth, or production, or money in the country as a whole, but upon unequal production and distribution and upon waste of wealth.*

Wealth is the product of labor—accumulations from gathering, producing, building, saving. Money is supplied as a convenient medium in exchanging labor's products. It constitutes but a small per cent of the total of wealth.

Poverty is lack of wealth. A poor man is one who from one or many causes does not have his proportion of the sum of labor's products.

It is a very superficial view of the case to conclude that it is more money that the poor man needs. He needs the material things which go to make for his comfort and happiness, and money is but a tool, sometimes used, in transferring these things from one to another— a means to an end.

It is a more superficial view to consider that it is a lack of money supply in the country at large that has caused depression among laboring classes. We have abundance of wealth in the country, but the laborer has not received his part of his own products. There is plenty for all, but the men and women who produce the wealth are robbed of their rightful share.

It is not a monopoly of money but rather a monopoly of wealth—the unequal distribution of labor's products—which is a chief cause of privation. And the question of money supply has very little to do as a factor in producing this inequality. I do not undertake to say whether there is or is not a sufficient volume of currency in the country, but I do undertake to say that any scarcity of money which now exists in the country is not a considerable cause of depression among laboring classes.

Besides, money is apparently scarce when there is a general lack of confidence in the ability or disposition of people to pay. No matter how much money there may be in any locality, or by whom held—whether by bankers, farmers or others—if there is lack of confidence in business conditions, men who have money are very cautious, as they should be, about loaning or investing it. When confidence in the integrity and success of business conditions is restored, money again freely circulates.

Do we need fifty dollars per capita? It has been assumed that we must require as large an amount of money in proportion to wealth and population as we ever did. This is not correct. In early days a large part of the business was done by the direct use of money. Now about ninety-five per cent of the business of the country is done by bank exchanges without the use of money. As business methods and facilities improve, and as business is done more and more upon a large scale, a smaller proportion of currency is required to transact the business. The largest volume of the country's business—manufacturing, mining, real estate, transportation, the wholesale trade—is done almost entirely by bank exchange. We probably do not use and do not need the amount of money per capita that we did forty years ago.

The most sagacious and enterprising business men use the smallest proportion of money in transacting business. Intelligent and prudent people keep but little money about their persons or homes. Their ready money, except what is barely sufficient for daily use, is deposited in bank, and bills are usually paid by check. As a rule, only those who are either stupid, ignorant, miserly, or who love display, do otherwise.

A burglar recently entered the residence of a Pasadena capitalist and secured one hundred and twenty-five dollars from the coachman's room. The coachman should have had better sense than to keep such an amount of money in his room. The man who habitually carries in his pocket more money than he needs for use—an amount of fifty dollars, for instance—is not wise ; in a business sense he is a fool.

Mechanics and others employed are usually paid by check at the end of the week or month, and do not usually carry much money. People who live farthest from a bank must needs keep on hand more money for use than those who have better bank facilities. The bank is a convenience and a money saver, and postal savings banks would be especially convenient in sparsely settled communities.

The amount of money, coin and paper, in the United States, is stated to be about twenty-five dollars per capita. We have those who advocate increasing the amount to forty or fifty or even one hundred dollars per capita. Most nations have a smaller amount of money per head than ours ; the United Kingdom about twenty dollars,

Germany, fourteen dollars ; Sweden and Norway, five dollars. A very few have more ; France, forty-two dollars; Netherlands, twenty-six dollars.

The proportion of money to population of a nation does not show the proportion of wealth or the condition of its people. It but shows the relative amount of money they are accustomed to use in the transaction of business. The wealth of a man can no more be told by the amount of coin in his pocket than by the style of his clothes ; and the same is true of a nation. J. J. Astor perhaps carries less money in his pocket than does his coachman. Some men like to carry as much of their wealth as possible in their pockets or on their backs, but sensible people usually carry as little as will answer their needs. The people of France, with a volume of currency of forty-two dollars per capita, are not more prosperous financially than are the people of England with only twenty dollars per capita.

It is a mistake to attribute the depression among agricultural and other laboring classes in some localities to a scarcity of money in the country at large. If that were a cause, it would affect manufacturing, mercantile and mining classes as well, but these have been usually prosperous and have accumulated wealth. As a whole the country has increased greatly in wealth, while, in many localities, farm lands have decreased in value in the past twenty-five years. We can account for the depression among agricultural classes while others have prospered, and scarcity of currency is not among the causes. Besides, the purchasing power of a dollar in buying the necessaries of life, is much greater than it was thirty years ago, and, consequently, much less currency is required to handle the same amount of goods.

Money should be issued by the national government in such quantity as may be required for the legitimate demands of business. We need not trouble ourselves with discussion of how much money we now have, in circulation or otherwise, or with the question of how much money we require per capita for the transaction of our business. No one knows or can know how much is needed per capita. That matter will take care of itself when we have accomplished the important feature of financial reform. Then the unfailing law of supply and demand will regulate that.

When the nation is the chief banker, with its branches throughout the country, the *amount* of currency will be easily adjusted by the legitimate requirements of business and trade.

CHAPTER XXX

LOANS UPON LANDS AND UPON FARM PRODUCTS. FREE COINAGE OF SILVER.

Let us see how it is proposed to increase the volume of currency, and how the money is to be placed in the hands of the people who need it. It is proposed to issue paper money and loan it upon the security of land and of non-perishable farm products.

Have we found that going in debt is a good way to secure financial betterment ? Is borrowing money, with or without security, the proper remedy to commend to poor people as a cure for poverty? Shall we advise them to put a mortgage on the farm? No! Borrowing money is one of the chief causes of the farmer's financial troubles, and borrowing more money is not his way out. Buying land on credit, and tools and machinery on credit, and horses, buggies, good clothes, groceries, pianos on credit, has been the bane of the farmer and of many other people. (Please read articles on "Speculation in Land," and "The Credit System.") And buying on credit, buying what one cannot pay for, putting a mortgage on the farm, are *not* the remedies for our poverty. Buying on credit and borrowing money produce an inflation of supposed wealth and values to the extent of the proportion of debt, and this leads us to think we are rich while we are poor. And we go on buying, using, consuming, expanding, wading more and more into the unknown waters of debt, speculation and expansion, until we lose our financial footing and see our goods and effects carried beyond our reach and we left without property and often without friends. No, keep on the solid ground of having something you can call your own, and owe no man or company of men for it.

Our past experience has also shown us that our financial disasters as a people have not been caused by contraction more than by expansion of the volume of currency. When it is easy for men to get money they spend it freely, and this is the case with communities as well as with individuals. Expansion of the volume of currency, in the judgment of some of our best statesmen, has, at several periods of our history, led to speculation, to increased business hazards and to financial ruin.

Another proposed plan for expanding the currency is by *"free and unlimited coinage of silver."* Silver is a very useful metal for coins of the denominations for which it is used. We need silver dollars, and should have as many as are needed for use. We now have over $300,000,000 silver dollars. Of these we use about $60,000,000. If we can use only one-fifth of the silver dollars we now have, why coin more ? We are told, in order to use them as a basis for notes or certificates. If for that purpose we would do better to use it as bullion than as coin.

Silver is properly used as a subsidiary coin, second to gold. No argument, no theory, no effort by the government or the people can make it otherwise. We use silver for money in amounts less than five dollars simply because the gold coin of less than five dollars is too small for use, just as we use nickel for a five-cent piece because the silver half dime is too small for use. The vast majority of people prefer to carry as little weight of coin as will answer their needs. Usually two or three dollars in silver is as much as any one takes from choice, and a man who would prefer to carry ten dollars in silver in his pocket unless it was needed directly for change would be a phenomenon. We do not need another silver dollar, and should not coin another until we can use those we have.

Besides, our standard silver dollar is not a dollar in fact. It is worth but seventy cents, and silver is still depreciating. It is because of the depreciation in the value of silver, owing to a large increase in the production of silver mines beyond the demand for their product, during the last three to four decades, that caused the demonetization of silver as a standard money in this and other countries, and which renders it impossible to fix a proportion of value between gold and silver. Silver is no longer coined in any country of Europe except as secondary coin.

Governments can not make values. They can but accept values as they find them. The value of gold, and silver, and iron; of wheat, cotton and corn and every other commodity produced by men, depends wholly upon supply and demand, and no power upon earth, except that of monopoly, can evade this inexorable law. A government puts its stamp upon a coin and says "this is a dollar," because the coin is, or should be, made of metal which is worth the amount, or nearly the amount stamped.

The stamp is the sign of government appraisement ; it has nothing to do with creating or fixing value to the metal used, except as the demand is increased by this use. Establishing a "legal tender" quality to the coin is entirely distinct from the actual value. Treasury notes are made legal · tender by government *fiat*, but coined money is used as a standard of value because it is, or should be, intrinsically worth what the stamp calls for, or very nearly as much. There is no good reason for making it otherwise except to cover the cost of coinage and handling. The lesser coins are very properly made less valuable.

For the United States to make a coin worth only seventy cents and call it a standard dollar is unwise—is a "false pretense" and unworthy our reputation as a nation composed of enlightened, substantial people, and having stable institutions. It is true that these silver dollars pass as well as gold, except for inconvenience of bulk and weight. Yes, they do for the same reason that our bank notes and treasury notes pass as readily as gold, simply *because all our money which is not gold is exchangeable for gold.* Our "coin of the realm" should be actually worth its face. Treasury notes are but "promises to pay." To coin a dollar which is seven-tenths value and three-tenths " promise to pay " is a nondescript money which should not be continued.

Besides, as it is true that the silver dollar is largely the money of the laboring classes—of those who work for a dollar or a dollar and a half a day, and buy the necessaries of life in corresponding amounts—that is the more reason, if any were needed, why the dollar coin should be actually worth a dollar. For labor is the producer of all wealth and should be paid in the very best money.

But, while these are grave objections, they are not the most serious ones to this proposed free coinage of silver, but it is the fact that this proposition is *a scheme to subsidize silver mine owners by a direct bounty of over forty per cent* on all the silver they can produce, which is the gravest objection. It is not so understood by the large number of farmers and others who advocate it as a means of relief from their present burdened condition. But the mine owners who meet in convention and resolve unanimously to insist upon free coinage of their product, very well understand what it means to them.

It is proposed that the nation shall buy all the silver which may be offered, paying for it in coined silver dollars or in silver certificates, on a basis of one dollar for an amount of silver equal to that in our silver dollar. That is to say, to pay one dollar for an amount of silver which is now worth less than seventy cents. And to buy all that is offered, on this basis.

But advocates of free coinage tell us that we do not propose to buy silver at all, but only to coin it for the mine owners.   That is a quibble.   *It is proposed to receive silver in exchange for silver dollars.*   If that is *not* buying, pray tell how we do when we buy?   And we would, of course, continue to exchange our gold for silver dollars with those who wished to exchange.

We have been subsidizing copper mine owners, and steel rail makers, and white lead trusts, and' in one way and another a great many other monopolists, but this is the boldest proposal yet, to pay a direct subsidy to a lot of millionaires as a means of relief for the distress of the toiling millions, and the proposal advocated by some of the toilers I   This would be decidedly a case of protection to an " infant " millionaire industry !

When the government needs silver for coin or for bullion it should continue to buy it in the market at the market price.   There is no good reason and there can be none why the nation should pay silver producers or any body else a price for their product greater than such articles are worth in the markets.   We should have *national* coinage of silver and of gold.   The *nation* should make and should issue all money and should have all the profit accruing therefrom, and *all the people*—not silver mine owners more than bankers—should receive the benefit.

CHAPTER XXXI

THE SUB-TREASURY PLAN. FIVE OBJECTIONS SET FORTH. LOANS UPON LAND SECURITY.

The proposed sub-treasury scheme has merits and demerits. The objections to it are, not that the government may not do a legitimate banking business, may not loan money to the people under proper conditions, but are, *1.* That money should not be loaned on any property security in as large proportion as eighty per cent of its value; *2.* Nor upon any farm product for a longer time than from three to six months; *3.* Nor at as low a rate of interest as 2 per cent ; *4.* Nor should the government make an issue of treasury notes for the sole purpose of loaning it to the people ; *5.* Nor should such issue be made at one season of the year to be cancelled at another. The proposition that the government loan money to the people on land security is also unwise.

1. *Loans should not be made upon any kind of property for more than one-half its value.* A loan of eighty per cent of the value upon farm products would in many cases be equivalent to purchasing the product. Such products are subject to frequent fluctuations in value. The price is liable to either increase or decrease at any time or season. Sometimes the price drops materially soon after a harvest. California dried peaches sold readily at twenty cents per pound from the ranches in October, 1890, and within sixty days could not be sold at

fifteen cents per pound.   Errors are liable in appraising values.   The cost of holding constantly adds to the amount of the loan.   As usual, the amount of the mort- gage surely and constantly grows, while the value of the property may not.   The legitimate province of loaning money does not include the probability of having to take the property in exchange for the money loaned.   What- ever business the nation undertakes to do, it should do in a business way, and the business of loaning money does not contemplate loaning such an amount upon property as would be liable to result in a purchase of the goods in payment of the loan.

2.   *Loans upon farm products should not be for a longer time than six months*, and better be for not over three months.

It is not usually good policy to hold farm products longer than a few weeks after they are ready for market, for an advance in price.   The cost of extra handling, storage, insurance, interest, shrinkage, and other losses, will usually more than offset any probable advance in price, if longer held.   While it frequently pays to hold for a short time for an advance, it is certainly not often wise to hold crops for six or nine months for a higher price.   Such holding tends to a cumulation of crops by piling one upon another, and would also, from the cost of holding, almost invariably result in loss.

Besides, the holding of property which one does not need, and which is not in itself growing in value, for an advance in price, is done upon speculation—gambling in futures—which is always delusive and dangerous, and the risk is greater in articles which are perishable (and most farm products are more or less so), and still more so where one owes for the property. And it would be very unwise on the part of the government to undertake, systematically, to encourage such speculative holdings by furnishing to an entire body of producers in several states the money with which to carry on such speculation.

3. *Money should not be loaned to the people at as low a rate as two per cent per annum.*

It is true that our government has issued some two per cent bonds, but they are not readily salable except to the national banks as a basis for their issue of notes. British Consols pay two and a half per cent, and that is the lowest rate at which any nation or corporate power can regularly obtain money. It is very evident that our government should not loan money at the lowest rate at which it can possibly borrow. The business of loaning money cannot be done without a profit any more readily than can the business of selling calico or potatoes be done without a profit. The rate of interest upon money, whether loaned by the nation, by a bank or by any one else, must depend upon supply and demand, and upon locality, amount, conditions, security and time.

The demand that the government shall loan money to the people at two per cent savors entirely too much of that socialism which demands something for nothing and which is not socialism but communism.

4. *The government should not make an issue of treasury notes for the sole purpose of loaning to the people.*

The first effect of such a general loan would be to make a sudden expansion of currency, to increase indebtedness, to increase business hazards, to encourage speculation, to inflate values, to induce lavish expenditures and extrav-

agant living, and to decrease farm production by decreasing the necessity for labor and increasing the proportion
of middlemen, speculators and gentlemen of leisure. The
secondary effect of such a loan would be a depreciation
of currency which would inevitably result in financial
disaster to the nation and in widespread loss and ruin
to many people. Temporary loans in moderate amounts
might be safely made, but not such loans by wholesale.

5. *The government should not issue treasury notes at one
season of the year to be cancelled at another,* unless new
issues were made to replace those cancelled, for the result
of periodic issues and cancellations would be to produce
frequent expansions and contractions of the currency
which could not be foreseen, and would operate to
unsettle financial and business affairs.

Loans on land security. The proposition to issue
treasury notes to be loaned to the people on land security
is open to all the objections of an issue to be loaned upon
farm products, and to other objections which do not
exist in the latter case.

The farmer's products are for sale. For him to obtain
a loan upon his products for a limited time in order
to enable him to effect an advantageous sale is not
open to serious objection. It is better for him to manage
without borrowing if he can, but it is at times excusable
or even desirable for him to borrow on his products.

*But the farmer's land is not for sale if he intends to con-
tinue to work the farm.* A mortgage is a sale. When the
farmer borrows money upon his land he sells his land to
secure payment of the loan, and then undertakes to
redeem it by paying the loan with interest. It is the
mortgages on the farms that we need to get rid of. The

farm mortgage burden should be lifted, and the hazardous, disastrous practice of mortgaging farms should be, as far as possible, abolished.

It is far better for a man to be a tenant farmer than to bear the burden of a heavily mortgaged farm. The man in the former condition is "as free as a bird" as compared with him who struggles under the load of a large mortgage. The care, the worry, the anxiety, the never ending toil, the scrimping and saving, the want and hardship of those who contend with the often almost hopeless task of paying a mortgage on the farm, will hurry a man or woman to an untimely grave faster than almost any other financial evil which could possibly beset them.

There are times when, as a result of adverse circumstances a man has got behind and is unable to carry on his business without a loan, it is best to make a loan on the farm. But a man should not begin with a mortgage, should not start out in that way, should not incur debt when it can possibly be avoided, should avoid expenditures which may lead to a mortgage, should avoid a heavy mortgage as he would a pestilence.

Should the government offer to loan money on lands to the amount of one-half their value, at four or five per cent on long time, the temptation to borrow would be too strong for very many people to resist, and there would be a large demand for the money. And an issue of the amount of money which would be called for would result in such an expansion of the currency as would inevitably, beyond the possibility of doubt, lead to much extravagance and speculation, and would end in a general financial panic, in widespread business disaster, and in poverty and want.

Going into debt, borrowing money upon land, speculation in land, needless expenditure and extravagant living,
are evils which should not be encouraged. Permanent
relief for the burdened laboring classes does not lie in the
direction of putting mortgages on their homes.

CHAPTER XXXII

*TAXATION—VARIOUS WAYS OF RAISING REVENUES—
SOME GENERAL PRINCIPLES FOR TAXATION.*

The methods of raising revenues in our country, are,
to a considerable extent, primitive, cumbersome and
unwise ; in many respects they are vicious—favoring the
rich and oppressing the poor.   In the matter of taxation
we have much to learn, and much room for improvement,
and in this direction we must look for ways and means
of lightening some of the present heavy burdens of our
industrial classes.

In order to raise money to defray the expenses of
government various means have been employed.   Taxes
have been levied upon imports and exports ; upon property of all kinds and upon persons ; upon luxuries and
vices ; upon business, incomes and legacies.   Nations
raise revenues from the ownership and conduct of mines,
fisheries, forests and other great natural opportunities ;
by the sale, lease or improvement of public lands ; by

the granting of franchises and other privileges ; by coining money and by banking ; by the construction and operation of canals, railways, bridges and other public works ; by conducting a mail service, telegraph service, and in various other ways.   Municipalities raise revenues by owning and operating gas, electric and water works, street car lines, and by constructing and operating other municipal improvements for public uses.

The most desirable, least burdensome, and least objectionable method of raising revenue for the support of government, is for the government to own and manage all public means of transportation and communication and other great public monopolies, and to derive a profit from carrying on such business.   This would be a decided improvement over any method of taxation.   This is a part of the advantages which should result from government ownership of railway and telegraph lines, of coal fields and of other mines and great natural opportunities for acquiring wealth.   Australia is leading the countries of the world in this as in some other great reforms, and is now deriving a part of the income needed for the support of its government by such means.   The German government derives an income from its railways and its coal mines.

Some general principles of taxation.   Until we become sufficiently enlightened and practical to raise the needed revenues for government support by wiser methods, we shall still be compelled to tax ourselves for that purpose, and we should adopt some wiser methods than now prevail in the nation and in many states of the Union.

1.   *Taxes should be so levied as to be paid by the people in proportion to their ability to pay them.*   Taxes are

usually levied at a uniform rate upon all property, regardless of its productiveness, of its utility or of the ability of the owners to pay. The farmer, the laborer, the common people, who are taxed upon all they possess and upon much of what they consume, pay a greater proportion of tax than do the rich, whose property is usually not as fully assessed and which to a much larger extent escapes taxation altogether. A tax upon articles consumed—upon the necessaries of life— bears especially heavy upon the poor, for a tax upon consumption, in the case of the poor who need to use all or nearly all their earnings to provide the necessaries of life, means a heavy tax upon nearly every dollar earned, while in the case of the rich it is a tax on only a very small part of their income.

Besides, in the case of taxes upon imports, higher rates are often charged upon articles of the most common necessity than upon those used as luxuries. Our tariff rates are higher upon common fabrics of cotton and wool, than upon finer ones of wool, fur and silk, and this is a serious objection to our present tariff.

There is a class of people who are either morally, intellectually or physically incompetent for respectable self support. Of this class are the dependents, paupers, criminals and others who are partly or wholly supported by state or private charity. Above this class—this "submerged tenth"—is a large number who are endeavoring, struggling—now succeeding and now failing—to provide for themselves and to be respectable, self-supporting citizens. Among these are the poor, the ignorant, the weak, the infirm, those who are not well employed or are poorly paid, those who have met with reverses or mishaps, those who have but little, and either have no homes of their own or very humble ones. To tax such people for any purpose is barbarous. Such should be assisted rather than hampered in their struggle for life.

It is a first duty of governments to protect and help the weak, to make it as easy as possible for men to be honest, upright, respectable, self-supporting, and to lay no burdens upon those who are unable to bear them. They should not be taxed. To tax such is oppression like unto the exactions of an absolute monarch of a portion of the substance of his toiling serfs.

An amount covering the value of an humble home should be exempt from the taxation of property used for a home, and an amount covering the value of the most necessary articles of household effects should also be exempt from tax. An exemption (of perhaps $800 to $1,200), varying in different states, should be made in the assessment of the home and its belongings, to the end that those who have so little shall not be taxed. Some states have such exemptions, but many have not. To exempt those who are unable to pay, or upon whom such payment would be a hardship not easily borne should be the first principle of taxation.

2. *Taxes upon property should be mainly upon the natural opportunities for acquiring wealth*, and not upon the products of labor—upon lands, mines, franchises ; not upon tools, machinery, improvements.

Land derives its value from the community, from the whole people, because of the presence, the labors, the needs of the whole. As the community gives value to the land, society as a whole, the state, should exact a large part of its revenues from the land. Every good citizen, by his residence, whether he have much or little property, adds value to the land in the locality where he resides. The town lots of the city and the lands in the country are valuable in proportion to the number of resident population and the general wealth of the people.

Aside from other reasons why land is and should be the chief subject of property taxation, this principle, that that which is made valuable by the whole people should pay tribute to the whole, is a sufficient reason why land should bear the principal burden of the property tax. And by a similar process of reasoning, that which the individual has made for himself, has accumulated by his labor and care, should be favored in the matter of taxation; should, as far as may be found practicable and equitable, be relieved from taxation.

Another and more important reason why lands and other natural opportunities should be made to bear the large share of property tax, and a reason based more upon practical and less upon ethical grounds, is, that a heavy tax upon lands, and especially upon unused lands, acts as a remedy for one of the great causes of poverty, waste and loss, speculation in land. This evil is so great, so widespread, so far reaching, so disastrous, so beyond all control from good morals or any other ordinary means, that we may well apply this as the only possible remedy for the evil. By making lands and city lots and mines and franchises pay a large part of the burden of taxation we shall certainly lessen the evils of land speculation. It would tend to the holding of land for use only.

It would also be a check upon land monopoly, upon the holding of land in large bodies by wealthy men and speculators to the injury of those who need land for use.

It would open the way for many people of small means who need a piece of land or a town lot for a home but cannot now obtain it, to secure what they need. And it would induce the holding of only so much land as one could well improve and bring to a high state of cultivation.

It is an evil in this country of much land, that many men hold more of it than they can profitably cultivate or otherwise care for. Fifty acres of land well tilled will usually bring a larger income than will one hundred acres poorly tilled, while saving the cost of fencing, cultivating and paying taxes on the larger tract. As a rule, in our country men try to hold and improve more land than they have the capital or labor to make profitable; and anything that could be done equitably to discourage the holding of unused or poorly used land, and to encourage a high state of cultivation, would make for the farmers comfort and independence.

The farmer is liable to think that the value of a town lot is small as compared with land for a farm. This is not the case. Desirable town lots cost about as much as desirable pieces of vacant land for farms, and it is about as difficult for a poor man in the city to obtain a good lot for a home as for the farmer to secure a good piece of ground for a farm; perhaps more so, as city lots are more often held upon speculation and above their value than is farming land. While the land of the farmer and of the city resident should be fully taxed, the tools, orchards, stock and fences of the farmer, the tools and machinery of the mechanic, and the goods and fixtures of the merchant and shop-keeper should be exempt from taxation. The direct product of labor, and especially the appli-

ances for use by the laborer, should be relieved from
taxation as far as practicable, while the burden of tax so
far as it is necessary to raise it from property may well
be borne by the land—man's natural heritage, a part of
which should be within the reach of every man that he
may provide himself with a home.

3. *Taxes upon property should be only on such property
as is tangible and may not easily escape assessment, and
should be upon the thing itself, and not upon mortgages,
stocks, bonds or other divided or separate ownership or token
of ownership.*

Land and fixed improvements upon the land—buildings,
railway tracks, telegraph lines, and other stationary
property—best answer this description, and are really
the only kinds of property which need be taxed. Such
property is readily found and must inevitably pay the
taxes levied, while personal property is often not so
easily found and much of it escapes taxation, so that
where personal property is taxed the burden is not uniform. Again, the value of real property for assessment
is fixed by the officials whose duty it is to place a value
upon it and these assessed values are uniform, while
personal property is usually valued for taxation by the
owners, and the assessed values vary with the varying
judgment and conscience of the different owners.

Again, the greater the number of articles taxed the
greater the cost of assessment and levy. And as a whole
the people are benefited by simplicity in the methods of
taxation.

In view of these and other reasons, most enlightened
nations no longer tax personal property. In this as in
many other things the people of this great republic are

behind the age. We have a very productive farm, but we have not, in many respects, learned how to properly till the farm, care for our estate or manage our household.

The government should not be concerned about the ownership of property assessed. It should look to the property and the property alone to pay the tax. No kind of property should pay more than one tax, and the person in possession should be held for that tax. There can be no possible advantage to any one from an assessment of stocks, bonds, mortgages and credits, and such a system adds to the cost, the annoyance, the vexation, the burden of the collection of taxes. The property *must* pay the tax. It is no relief to the owner to have his debt upon the property assessed to his creditor. The owner must foot all the bills.

We should tax a railway company and a farmer in the same manner. Tax *the property* of the company, not its stocks and bonds. The *road* is the source of all wealth of the company and must pay everything—taxes, interest on bonds, dividends on stock, etc. And there is no advantage to the farmer in taxing the mortgage on his farm. The farmer or the farm must ultimately pay all the charges—taxes, interest, insurance, assessments and costs of whatever kind, and the government cannot assist him by assuming to elect that his creditor shall help to pay his taxes.

A tax upon realties—upon land and fixed improvements upon the land, comes nearest to answering all the requisites for the basis of a simple, uniform, impartial, economic, sufficient property tax. It is true that objections may be raised to such a basis of taxation, but greater objections exist to any other system of property taxation.

CHAPTER XXXIII

NECESSITY FOR AN INCOME TAX. EXPERIENCE OF OTHER COUNTRIES. OBJECTIONS CONSIDERED.

Taxes should be laid upon incomes as well as upon property. No tax upon property alone. of few or many kinds, is sufficient as a basis for a uniform, complete, impartial system of taxation.

There is a large proportion of people who have little property but have good incomes, and are well able to pay and should pay their full share of tax burdens, and yet who, under our present system, are almost or entirely exempt from taxation. Among this class are those working upon salaries in the employment of government, of railway, telegraph, manufacturing or other corporations; men engaged in real estate, insurance, and many other kinds of business, and who have good incomes, who live well, spend money freely and take the world easy, but who acquire little property, and under our system do not at all, in proportion to ability, bear their share of the cost of government support. In this respect " They toil not, neither do they spin." They receive the full benefit of the social compact and bear no part of the expense of maintaining it. It does not require the ability of a great statesman to see that in this regard our system is defective. Here is a young man in railway employ receiving

$1,200 a year and spending it all and paying no taxes. And here a mechanic working for $2 a day who is assessed $1,000 upon his property and pays $25 yearly taxes.

Then there are many rich people who have large incomes, derived from mining, banking, manufacturing, transportation or other lucrative business, and whose payment of taxes from property assessments is not at all commensurate with their ability to pay.

A tax upon incomes is in fact the most equitable system of taxation which can possibly be devised, because the amount of income received by each individual is the best measure of his ability to bear a share of the expense of government. And a tax upon incomes alone forms a much better system of taxation than that upon property only.

For half a century the revenues of the United Kingdom have been raised mostly by a tax upon incomes and with no property tax. Switzerland and Prussia also have income taxes. And these taxes are uniformly approved by the people of these countries and are fully established as a settled principle of government.

The question arises, " Why then do we not adopt a system of income taxes?" There are several reasons. The leading one is that an income tax would compel capitalists to pay their proportion of taxes, consequently they do not favor such a tax, and, as usual, the interests of the rich rather than of the poor are considered by many of our modern politicians. Again there is our honored system of prohibitory tariff taxes, and the prohibitory party, especially, denounces any proposed plan of raising revenues which might perchance interfere with the benign operations of our high tariffs. And from these premises it follows that the political papers and leaders working for party success and in the interest of corporations and capitalists find ready arguments in opposition to this as to other proposed reforms.

The objections usually raised to an income tax are that it is "inquisitorial," would make the assessor a spy upon every man's business, accounts and affairs ; that it acts as a premium upon dishonesty and perjury, and bears hardest upon the honest man; and that our high spirited, free, independent American citizens will *never* submit to such a law I

Those who make such objections do not see, or at least do not call attention to the fact, that these objections hold in a greater degree against all taxes upon personal property. The citizen is catechised as to the value of his household goods, his beds, bedding, kitchen utensils, his money, notes, credits, pigs, poultry, watches and every earthly thing which he possesses. And is this not "inquisitorial ? " And do not the dishonest, in assessing such property, cover up as much as possible the extent and value of their possessions? And does this not act as a premium upon perjury ?

All such objections against an income tax may be made with greater force against a tax upon personal property. And how about tariff taxes? Are not they "inquisitorial?" No other tax system calls for such rigid question and search of one's baggage, clothing, personal effects and even of one's person. How is that for inquisitorial ?

These objections would not be valid or admissible in the case of those employed upon salary, nor would it in most other cases be as difficult to determine the one item of income as it would to find the ownership and fix the value of a long list of goods, wares, chattels and effects.

In all of these particulars it is easier, more simple, more practicable to arrive at a just and uniform assessment of the value of incomes, taking the people as a whole, than to equitably assess their personal property. And the most of those who object to an income tax do not object to the personal tax.

However, granting that there would be difficulty in rightly assessing the value of incomes in a certain proportion of cases, just as there is in an assessment of personalties, the fact will still remain that there is a large proportion of people who are abundantly able to pay a full share of the cost of government maintenance, but who now escape bearing their part of this burden and will continue to do so until we adopt an income tax, and the fact remains that there can be no equitable system of taxation which does not include the income tax.

The income tax should not be made a double tax. The individual should not be taxed on his income and equally on property from which the income is partly or wholly derived. The amount of tax upon the farm, the mill, the store, the shop or other property from which income is derived should be deducted from the amount of tax upon income.

Some writers upon this subject contend that there should be no deductions from the amount of income tax on account of any tax upon property from which the income is derived. They reason that a tax upon incomes is a measure of relief to those who are taxed upon property, because it compels many to pay taxes who have no property, or to pay in excess of their property tax, and, consequently, that those who are benefited by this tax should not object if under the new system they are required to pay their proportion of the income tax, as well. It is clear that an income tax acts as a measure of relief to those taxed upon property, but we cannot see that this is a reason why those who have property should be doubly taxed in order to reach those who have none. Such taxation would tend to make the holding of property unprofitable, and would discourage the owning of property.

One advantage of an income tax is, that it favors the holding of property by placing a share of tax burdens on those who have no property and thus lessens the burdens of those who have homes of their own.

The tax on incomes should be only on the surplus over an amount required for a comfortable living of a family in humble circumstances. A reasonable exemption, in most states, would probably be $500, of income, not subject to tax.

CHAPTER XXXIV

*A TAX ON INHERITANCES. ADVANTAGES OF SUCH
A TAX.*

Wealth is omnipotent. It dominates all interests. It rules in social, in business and in state affairs. The will of the man who counts his wealth by millions is often more potent in deciding affairs of the community and of the state than is the voice of a thousand men who are dependent on their daily toil for support.

The aggressive power of the men of great wealth, who, to a large extent, control transportation, manufacturing, mining and other great industries ; who form oil, sugar, beef and other trusts and dictate the prices of the necessaries of life ; and who so largely dominate in the enactment and administration of the laws, has come to be a great tax upon the industries, a drain upon the wealth, and a bar to the progress of the laboring classes, and is a menace to the success of popular government.

This grave evil, the accumulation of vast wealth in the hands of a few men, is being constantly augmented by the transmission of these accumulations from generation to generation, thus perpetuating a monied class, an aristocracy of wealth, which is not in harmony with American character or with our Republican institutions.

The founders of this great Republic set out to establish a true Democracy, a nation ruled by its common people, where the laws should be in the interest of all, where no class should have special favors and where aristocrats should be unknown.

They sought to found a nation where the common people should not be ruled and oppressed by a king and nobility who assumed entire ownership of the land and full power to rule over their fellow men, and whose power was perpetuated by the entail of assumed ownership and authority from the father to the oldest son. And they thought to insure the people from the domination of an aristocracy by abrogation of the law of primogeniture. But, in these latter days, a new aristocracy has arisen—an aristocracy of wealth, which, like the landed and titled aristocracies of Europe, is dominant and oppressive, and measures are demanded to abate this aggressive power.

This is one of the problems with which we are confronted. We may enact laws, institute reforms and inaugurate enterprises by the state, tending to produce more nearly an equilibrium of wealth production and distribution. But what shall we do to curtail the power of the aristocracy which now exists, and which, under our laws, is being perpetuated and increased in numbers and in power? How shall we place limits upon enormous aggregations of wealth in few hands? There should be some method of putting limitations upon the power of the "dangerous wealthy classes," and though we may not restrict legitimate acquisitions, we can at least limit the transmission of large accumulations, and this may be done properly and effectively by a graduated tax upon estates.

Besides, as elsewhere shown, much of the wealth of millionaires is not the result of legitimate earning and saving. It has been drawn from its rightful sources by exorbitant charges for public service, by exactions from labor, by abstractions from the public domain, by monopoly, jobbery and plunder. Much of this wealth belongs of right, to the people who produced it, and a tax upon estates would be a measure of compensation.

The rights, the property, the liberty of the individual are always subject to the interests of the community. The interests of society are paramount to those of the individual. The city or state confiscates or prohibits the use of the property of the brewer, the tanner, the soap maker, the butcher, when such use is deemed prejudicial to the interests of the community. The state prescribes rules for the possession and right use of property. At every step in life, in endeavoring to carry out our own desires are we met by the requirements of the state.

If the state prescribes conditions under which a man may acquire and transfer property during his life, it more narrowly specifies what may be done with his property after his death. Testamentary rights are often much limited. The state may well prescribe what may be done with a man's estate after his death, and from no other source may it look for a provision for a considerable part of its revenues with less probability of hardship to any one, or with as much benefit to the community, as from a scaled tax upon estates, and especially by a heavy tax upon estates of millionaires. And in this way may we place some restriction upon the perpetuation of our aristocracy of wealth.

This could be done without hardship or burden to any one, and by a just, wise and beneficent use of the powers and prerogatives of the state. In this way could be effected an ample provision of funds for schools, libraries, hospitals, reformatories and for many other benevolent state purposes and beneficial public improvements. It would also act as a relief to the poor from the burden of taxation, and to reduce taxes upon realties. It would lessen the incentive to the acquisition of great fortunes and be an incentive to men of wealth to devote much of their means and energies to humanitarian labors and to make benevolent bequests during life. It would tend to improve the financial conditions of the poor and middle classes by a partial redistribution of accumulated wealth. And it would act as a restriction upon the aggressive and dangerous power of the very wealthy classes, and to lessen the extent of our aristocracy of wealth by reducing the amount transmitted from parent to child.

A graduated tax upon estates should be premised by

certain exemptions. All estates of those dying possessed of but a moderate amount of wealth, such an amount as would be required as a reasonable provision for the family and dependent friends of the decedent, should be exempt from tax. In making allowance for exemption, the conditions and needs of those dependent upon the estate should be considered.

As a suggestion to illustrate the principle here advocated, the following scale is presented:

Estates valued at less than $20,000, to be exempt from taxation.

Estates valued at

$20,000 to	$100,000	to pay a	10	per cent tax
100,000 to	500,000	"	15	"	"
500,000 to	5,000,000	"	20	"	"
Over	5,000,000	"	25	"	"

In each case the lesser rates to apply on the lesser amounts, and in each case liberal provision for dependent persons to be made, precedent to the tax.

Such a tax on estates, like a tax on incomes will not, as a rule, be advocated by the wealthy classes. Nor can we expect the ordinary politician or party leader to advocate such a measure, but rather to denounce it as a measure of state confiscation, and as being in the direction of communism. Nevertheless, the principle is correct and will find plenty of able advocates.

PART IV.

AFTERMATH. RESULTS AND LESSONS OF
THE CAMPAIGN OF 1892. THE POLIT-
ICAL OUTLOOK

CHAPTER XXXV

A TIME FOR COUNCIL AND A TIME FOR WAR. SOME
QUESTIONS SETTLED. AN OBSTACLE REMOVED.
A REFORM THAT LANGUISHES

I intended to have had this work published before the opening of the political campaign of this year, but, not having sufficient time to give to the matter, was disappointed in this. I hoped that my labors might, in a small way, help in the canvas to further the progress of some needed reforms.

But it is perhaps as well for the success of my work that the publication was delayed. During a political campaign, the ordinary citizen is a partisan. He " belongs to " one of the contending armies. He stands for the platform and the candidates of his party. He does not allow himself to admit that there are weaknesses in the position of his party, or that other parties have merits which his has not. He is not, for the time, an independent thinker, or an unbiased advocate. He does not, for the time, permit himself to assist any cause which is not in harmony with the aims of his party, or which may jeopardize its success.

There is a small contingent of independent thinkers and voters who are at all times ready to help a good cause. During a campaign this number is reduced to a minimum, but when the campaign is over, the proportion of partisans decreases, and the ordinary citizen is much more ready to listen to the advocates of measures which have been opposed or not adopted by his party. During the late campaign the proportion of independent thinkers was much larger than in the previous ones, and since the dimensions of the political landslide have become known there are great accessions to the ranks of those who are seekers after the true and the right way in political affairs. So that my opinions upon political problems will doubtless be better received by a majority of those who give them a consideration than they would have been during the campaign.

Besides, it affords opportunity to note the lessons, the results and the probable consequences of the campaign ; the work already accomplished ; the obstacles in the way of progress practically removed ; and to consider the prospects of questions and of parties in the future.

Some work accomplished. One legislative reform, the benign effects of which have been apparent in nearly every state of the Union, is now an accomplished fact. The Australian ballot has come to stay. In most cases the reform is complete ; in some cases correction is needed. The adoption of this reform, against the opposition of many leading politicians, marks an era in the progress of popular government. It puts us a long way on the road toward reaching a clean ballot, and an honest, economic and efficient conduct of public affairs.

No party is entitled to any special credit for inaugurating this reform. It was quite generally opposed by the politicians and the bosses, but was upheld by the intelligent, thinking masses The American nation should doff its hat to the Australian government for this pronounced reform which it has given us without charge for copyright.

Another legislative reform which is of even greater importance than ballot reform, and which is now fairly before the American people, and which is coming rapidly and coming to stay, is the decree that *intelligence shall rule* throughout the land and that ignorance shall take a back seat. The people of California voted almost unanimously at the late election in favor of an educational qualification for voters ; requiring that each voter shall be able to read and write in the English language.

This reform will relieve us of much of the incubus of ignorance and vice with which the body politic is weighted, and will make it much easier to carry needed reforms by appeals to the judgment and conscience of intelligent voters. The ignorant, bigoted, superstitious, depraved— foreign or native born—black, brown or white, will not much longer hold a balance of power which is largely wielded in the interest of a corrupt management of public affairs. . The Australian ballot and the educational qualification for voters, together, will do much to lift us out of the " slough of despond " in which we have been held by the degrading influence and power of ignorant and venal voters. They will to a great extent counteract the vicious influence of the slum vote.

And still another legislative reform which has been advocated for several years by a handful of reformers, the election of United States Senators (and Presidents, as well,) by direct vote of the people, in the late campaign for the first time received substantial endorsement.

California pronounced for this reform. *It, too,* is coming and with little opposition. And then millonaires will no longer buy places in our upper house.

Also, during the late canvas the question of restricting undesirable immigration received more attention than ever before. It is now fairly before the people and will be considered without much delay.

Not only have we made progress toward the adoption of some of these minor reforms, but that greatest obstacle in the way of success of the greater political reforms (unless we except party prejudice)—the tariff question, which has been the dominant issue in American politics for the past two to three decades, monopolizing the attention of the people almost to the total exclusion of all other questions, has at last received its death blow as an issue. The campaign of 1892 will relieve the nation of the incubus of monopoly tariffs and of the incubus of the tariff question as a monopoly issue in politics, as well.

This issue has been as a solid wall, blocking the way of progress. For many years have the advocates of moral and economic reforms been hoping for the extinction of this question as an issue, and there is great rejoicing all along the line of reformers at the good prospect of its final demolition. Questions that are of the utmost importance to us will now receive attention. We will have new issues. Those who have been blind will be made to see the light.

Oh ! The skies *are* brightening. Dawn is near. And the day will see many workers in the fields of human progress, and our labors will be crowned with a goodly measure of success.

But there is an administrative reform—that long-looked-for, much-hoped-for, but almost-despaired-of reform of the civil service, in which we have made but little progress. The great parties have declared for it, but their administrations have failed in practice to give it substantial recognition. They have encouraged us much, but disappointed us grievously. This reform languishes in the house of those who claim to be its friends, and it remains in a feeble and drooping condition. Reforms dependent upon administration appear to be much more difficult of consummation than are those which are mostly legislative.

Perhaps the incoming administration will gather some inspiration from the oncoming host of reformers, and will seek to merit commendation from the people by giving us a much better civil service than we have before seen. We may reasonably expect to see an improvement in this respect during the next four years. But, whether we be gratified by such an advance or not, we shall look with confidence to the new party which is soon to be marshaled in the cause of reform, and is to assume the management of our public affairs, to give us a genuine and complete reform of our government service, and to entirely abolish the demoralizing spoils system and relieve us of the evil effects produced by it upon our government and upon our political life.

The campaign of 1892 was conducted in much better form than previous ones. It was more wholesome, decent and respectable. It was more a campaign of education. There was more of genuine reason and argument ; more readiness to listen to speakers of the opposite parties ; more deference paid to the political opinions of others.

There was less of personal mud slinging ; less of noise and parade ; less of cannon, banners and torches. So that, in many respects, the late campaign was a decided improvement over previous ones, and marked an era of better things in politics.

CHAPTER XXXVI

THE POLITICAL PARTIES. THEIR POLICY IN THE CAMPAIGN OF 1892. REPUBLICAN. DEMOCRATIC. PROHIBITION. PEOPLES.

The Republican Party has now had almost continuous control in the councils of the nation for nearly a generation. It came into power as the champion of the cause of the oppressed. It was formed for a great purpose, and it was the leader and chief factor in accomplishing a great work. It stood for human liberty and equality, and for the preservation of the Union of States. It has been truly a grand party, and a party of reform. Its principles have been advocated by a long line of illustrious patriots and statesmen.

Since the completion of the special work for which the Republican Party was organized, it has come to be, more than any other party, the advocate and champion of monopoly, especially in manufacturing, mining and banking. In the outset this was done for what appeared to be for the best interests of the country and the masses of the people, and its policy was very generally approved. But a majority of the American people have discovered that subsidizing one class of people at the expense of another class, and especially that subsidizing capitalists at the expense of the common people, is not a good policy in this or in any other country. And the party which has come to be the subsidy party is no longer at the front in American politics.

The old party has been staggering under a load of legislation in the interest of monopoly, and in consequence of this load it suffered from serious disasters in 1890 and has met its Waterloo in 1892. It must go down along with the collapse of extremely high tariffs and other monopolistic agencies which it has fostered. And no party will again be so foolhardy as to take up the load which has broken the back of the grand old party.

Democratic Party. The Democratic Party had been for many years the conservative party in American politics, uniformly opposing innovations and reforms. Its character in this respect had been well established. But when the Republican Party changed its attitude, from having been the exponent of true democracy, to being the champion of monopoly and plutocracy, the Democratic party, as opposing high tariffs and other methods of subsidy, came to be, for the time, a reform party—the champion of a much needed reform of the tariff. And the Democratic Party has in the main been gaining the ground and the prestige which has been lost by the Republican Party.

And so the Democratic Party in 1892 has swept the field and gone into power with a strong majority over all, and will have full sway in the national and in the majority of state governments. This Democratic avalanche does not mean that the party has undertaken to champion any new reforms, or that its policy, excepting upon the one issue along which the great mass of forces was aligned in the campaign of 1892, is approved by a majority of the American people.

The great Democratic victory of 1892 means that there was wide dissatisfaction with the existing monopolistic order of things, for which the Republican Party was held largely responsible, and that the Democratic Party was used, for the time, as presumably the most available agency for expressing that dissatisfaction. It stands as the verdict of the American people against extremely high tariffs, and against a force bill, extreme pension measures, and a " federal brigade " in politics, as well.

It does not mean that a majority of the people have joined their political fortunes with the Democratic Party simply because they are dissatisfied with the Republican regime, and agree, in the main, with Democratic ideas of tariff reform. Happily, the tariff question has been " fought to a finish," and will not again be an issue in American politics. And the great body of intelligent voters who have heretofore been held in Republican or Democratic camps by this minor question as a forced issue, will now be ready to undertake the cause of more important reforms.

The Democratic Party has been and still is the con-servative party of this country, but, as opposing the extremely high tariffs enacted by the Republican Party, it is in that respect the reform party. The reform ele-ments are unitedly opposed to a high tariff policy, and very many of these voted a Democratic ticket in 1892 to help give that policy its deathblow. But, this issue aside, the Democratic Party will again assume its normal position as the great conservative party, and in a new organization of political forces, all opponents of reforms will there find a congenial political home.

The Democratic Party being also the pronounced opponent of all " sumptuary " laws, and the tried friend of the saloon, in a new political alignment prohibitionists from both old parties must join the party of reform, and the saloon forces will go to the Democratic Party. And so we may expect to see this old conservative and anti-sumptuary party remain in the field and gather in all the opponents of economic and of moral reforms.

The Prohibition Party. The force of the Prohibition Party as a factor in politics is not to be measured by its numbers. Prohibitionists are, as a rule, more zealous and active in propagating their principles than are the members of the old parties. The number of those who favor prohibition far exceeds the number of those who adhere to the party, and there is a large number outside the party who wish it success. Many thousands of Democrats and Republicans would have joined the Prohibition Party but for the strength of old party prejudice and affiliation.

Members of the Prohibition Party in all states where it is well organized are the principal advocates of prohibition, and are leaders in all prohibition contests and in all other moral contests, as well. In the intelligence, sobriety and moral standing of its membership, the Prohibition Party holds first place.

As a moral force in politics the Prohibition Party has no competitor ; it is the only party with a moral issue. It is the only party which openly opposes that great political crime —license of the liquor traffic, and the only party which stands unequivocally for equal political rights for women.

The Prohibition Party, as now constituted, has two serious defects ; 1. Its platform is too narrow on its main question, and, 2. It assumes a religious character. This party is the special champion of prohibition of the liquor traffic, yet, according to its platform, it is only ready to work for this when it can be done by states or by the nation. And many advocates of the principles of the party contend that " local option " is a snare and a device of the enemy, that it is not effective or satisfactory, that it " relieves the consciences of voters " and keeps them from working for the larger measure of reform, and that to work for such a half-way measure is to compromise with evil.

We have a large area of territory under absolute and well enforced prohibition through local laws. True prohibitionists, everywhere, are ready to work for prohibition in any contest that is on, whether in a town, a county or a state. In California, since Pasadena has established the right of local prohibition under the state constitution, members of the Prohibition Party have been active in many localities of the state in working for prohibition by towns and by counties, and a large area has been brought under prohibition, and no one would think of undertaking a contest for state prohibition until a much larger proportion of the people have declared for the principle in a local way. Several of the states, as Massachusetts and Mississippi, have adopted a policy of local prohibition, with a steadily increasing area voting " dry." Several cities of Massachusetts made a decided advance for the prohibition cause in the late election, even Boston coming within a few hundred votes of pronouncing for prohibition.

The dividing line between the contending forces on the liquor traffic question falls between license and prohibition, and a political party which opposes license should stand for prohibition, anywhere and everywhere, and always be ready for a contest where there is a reasonable prospect of success. The platform of a Prohibition Party should be in accord with the action of the great body of Prohibitionists throughout the country, on the question of prohibition. The old parties, as a rule, declare for license. The Prohibition Party should have room for all who oppose license : it should stand for prohibition by towns and by counties, by states whenever it can be compassed, and by the nation wherever it holds jurisdiction in local affairs.

Most of the work for temperance, as for other moral reforms in this country has been led by religious bodies or under religious auspices. Probably a majority of prohibition workers are church members. It is therefore not strange that prohibition meetings have been usually conducted with religious exercises.

But we should remember that we are proud to claim our land as the home of religious as well as of civil liberty, and we should remember that our nation does not guarantee religious liberty to Christians only. The Puritans sought "the wild New England shores" to secure for themselves the blessing of religious liberty, yet denied that privilege to others, and we have many good people to-day who, in their zeal for what they deem proper religious observance, ignore the rights of those who hold other religious views.

Temperance or other moral reform work in a social way may be properly and laudably carried on with an observance of religious forms or ceremonies. But a political party in this country in order to be in harmony with our free institutions, and to deserve success, must have room on its platform and in its councils for Jews, Infidels, Pagans and Christians.

The National Prohibition Convention of 1892 made a serious mistake in declaring for a pronounced free trade policy. A sudden change of policy on the tariff question from our present extremely high tariffs to the other extreme of free trade would be a very unwise course for the nation to adopt. Happily, we are not at all likely to have such a wide change in tariff legislation in the immediate future.

The People's Party. The People's Party is the leader of the new sociological movement in American politics. In some states it has shattered the monopolistic forces, and is in a fair way to go in and possess the land. It has achieved a phenomenal success for a new party. It has sent its representatives to state capitals and to the Halls of Congress. The "voice of the people" is to be heard in the councils of the nation. It stands as the avowed exponent and champion of economic reforms. In the late campaign it was the only party which stood, unequivocally, for the great principle of national ownership of railway and telegraph lines, and it has accomplished much in educating the people on this question. As the maker of the reform party of the future it holds a leading place.

Still, the People's Party is but a forerunner—but a "John the Baptist," of the reform party that is to be. In some respects it is unwise and extreme, and in some it is, unwittingly. untrue to its position as the avowed

opponent of monopoly. The demands expressed by some
of its leaders for "transportation at cost" and "money
at cost," sounds communistic. But it is common for
leaders of reform to take radical grounds, and we should
probably take such expressions as meaning that the
people want, and intend to have, transportation, and
money, and clothing, and tools, and the necessaries
of life, at living rates, and that the era of exorbitant
charges is near its end.

The People's Party in the campaign of 1892 made two
rather serious mistakes, 1, it did not give the great question of economic reform—government ownership—the
leading place in its platform or in its canvas, and, 2, it
made its fight mainly on a demand for cheaper money, to
be secured by loans from the government at two per cent,
and by the free and unlimited coinage of silver.

Nearly all things that are worthy of consideration in
questions of financial reform are embodied in the great
principle of *national ownership* of all great monopolies—
of money as well as of transportation. Money *cannot*
be loaned at two per cent, and free coinage of silver is a
device of the enemy—a scheme of monopolists. Questions
of methods and rates of loans, and of plans for an increase
of currency, are but questions of ways and means in
carrying on a great service, and these do not involve the
main principle which is, or should be, the ground of our
contention.

And, while it is probably true that these financial
questions, as presented, were drawing cards for the People's
Party in the late campaign, yet they are comparatively
secondary and transitory, and the silver question is very
largely one of local self-interest. The inducement which

carried Colorado for the People's Party in 1892, was the same in character as that which has been the chief inducement to keep Pennsylvania in the Republican column— the self-interest of silver producers in the one case, and of iron producers in the other. And the American people can no more be depended on to stand for the financial aggrandizement of silver barons, than of iron kings, at their own cost. Not when they know it.

Notwithstanding, the People's Party contains a large part of the leaven which shall leaven the whole lump, and form the great, new party of the future.

CHAPTER XXXVII

A NEW POLITICAL PARTY. NECESSITY FOR IT.
WHAT IT SHOULD STAND FOR. QUESTIONS
THAT ARE URGENT.

The coming party should be built mainly on the great coming issue—*State co-operation*—national, state and municipal ownership of the great monopolies. The reforms demanded in transportation, communication currency, land, are all comprehended under this principle. It comprises the sum and substance of the sociological movement in politics. It is *the* economic question of the day, and it can almost be said that there is no other. This is the distinctive feature of the new politics as contrasted with the old.

State ownership is the remedy for burdensome taxes, for exorbitant charges, for labor troubles, for strikes and lockouts, for monopolies and trusts. It would bring work to idle hands and food to hungry mouths. The great upheaval in our political life, the great cry for economic reform, means just this. Nothing less will satisfy the demand. Nothing else will bring the relief. It is to be the issue, and it is to remain as such until this reform becomes an established principle of our national life.

The one other great question is the moral one—prohibition of saloons, lotteries, gambling dens, brothels. The success and perpetuity of modern civilization depends upon the promotion of intelligence and virtue and upon the suppression of vice; and it is a chief duty of the state to foster the one and to suppress the other. For the state to sanction and legalize schools of vice, and thus to be itself the promoter of crime, is a paradox in government and a perversion of every right principle of law. There can be no darker political crime than for the state to license vice and thus to encourage and foster crime. Not many decades can pass until our people will look back upon this dark age in wonderment that it was possible for good, well meaning people, to uphold such a crime by voice or by vote.

The moral reform is of no less importance than the economic one, nor does it hold any second place in the minds and hearts of a majority of our people. But there are potent reasons why, as a political issue, the economic question will come to the front. It will do so as a part of the inevitable logic of political events.

The moral reform is not new, nor untried. The principle of prohibition as the only adequate remedy for vice, is fully established in the minds of a very large number of our people. The reform has become in many instances a part of our statute or organic code, and the results of these laws as promotive of good order and good citizenship are among the things of our written history.

In Maine, Iowa, Kansas, Vermont, Massachusetts, Mississippi, the Carolinas and Dakotas, and in other states, the principle of prohibition is established as the law of the land and is growing in favor with the people. This reform is steadily advancing and will not go backward. For a generation have philanthropists been zealously laboring to establish this reform. Every argument has been used. The people are familiar with every phase of the question. And now that these efforts have been crowned with so large a measure of success, we may well afford to give a considerable part of our time to the establishing of the principles of economic reform. *This harvest, too, is great, and the laborers are few.* Nor need we lessen our zeal for the one while we undertake the other.

The great economic question is of first importance because *it* also vitally concerns the comfort, the well being, the happiness, the health and the life of millions of our people ; because it more directly appeals to the masses, who are in sore need through no fault of their own, than does any other question ; because it is for these masses more directly a question of bread and of meat, of clothing and of shelter, than is any other ; and because, *while it is a reform most urgently demanded, it has as yet received but a very small comparative measure of attention from our people.*

While we have been contending over tariffs, high or low ; while we have been fostering corporate monopolies and most graciously submitting to their exactions ; while we have been nursing sectional prejudice, and submitting to boss rule ; we have been blind, deaf and dumb ; we have been densely ignorant and foolishly oblivious of the importance of these great economic reforms. We had but to look to England, and to Austria, and to Germany —those " effete monarchies "—to have learned lessons in state co-operation, and to see the advantages of state railways and state telegraphs.

Regarding the expediency of a national party espousing the prohibition cause, there are two principal factors to be considered : 1. There is a large proportion, perhaps a majority, of our people, who favor the principle of prohibition and are committed to the reform, and this proportion is constantly growing. Reforms do *not* go backward. And to stand for the *principle* of prohibition, would be an element of strength and not of weakness to a new party which was sound on other questions.

2. The church people are almost a unit for the principle of prohibition. Nearly all of the conventions of the religious bodies have pronounced unequivocally in opposition to license and in favor of prohibition. It is true that thus far but a minority of church membership have shaped their political course in accordance with church edicts. But we must make large allowance for the alleged importance of that most wonderful tariff question, and for the strength of party prejudice. We may reasonably hope that the political revolution of 1892 will release some millions of church members from the strong bonds of the tariff issue and of party prejudice, and that the great body of church members will be able in the near future to clearly see the plain duty which lies before them as Christian citizens in regard to the saloon evil.

The statesman, in considering the future of political parties, should understand that church people are bound, sooner or later, to stand as a solid body with the political party which openly opposes the saloon and its kindred evils. There can be no mistake about this. *The church and the saloon are deadly enemies,* and no man or woman can long hold a place in the ranks of the one while giving aid and comfort to the other. It cannot possibly be otherwise. The church is the leading agency in promoting moral reforms; and its members can occupy no equivocal or double position toward this greatest of all evils, this chief promoter of vice. And the politician who plans a new political party which has no ground upon which a Christian or Jew can consistently stand, surely " reckons without his host."

The Democratic Party will stand as it has stood as the friend and protector of the saloon and the brothel, as "opposed to all sumptuary laws which vex the citizen," and as in favor of the fullest license for the gratification of appetite and passion. And the new party must stand, not only for state monopoly as opposed to private or corporate monopoly, but also for the suppression of saloons, brothels and gambling dens.

There is but one other great question. It is a question of human equality—of human rights and privileges. It is the question whether one-half of the people—one-half of the thinkers and toilers—shall continue to enact the laws and conduct the government, regardless of the voice, the needs, the rights, of the other half. It is the question whether woman shall have those political and civil privileges which of right belong to her and have been so long withheld. It is a matter of simple justice, and also a necessity for the promotion of good morals and of good government.

The People's Party, in some states, has declared for equal suffrage, and as a national party it can illy afford to deny the right of woman to an equal voice in state affairs, inasmuch as the party very largely owes its success to the labors and the influence of women. The Prohibition Party, and nearly all prohibitionists, are in full accord with this reform. The Knights of Labor, and most other industrial organizations, are in favor of political equality without regard to sex.   The best citizens of all parties are coming to recognize the importance of woman as a factor in politics, and the injustice of denying political rights to her.

The sentiment in favor of granting political equality to woman is constantly growing among the people, several states have, in whole or in part, extended to her the right of franchise, and a *reform* party which ignores this reform, is behind the age.   It is not " keeping up with the procession."

There are *three great political problems* ; the economic, the moral, and that of human equality.   All other questions are secondary, and follow, in principle, as the inevitable sequence of these.   The most of them are already either endorsed by a large proportion of the people, or are being advocated with a steadily growing sentiment in their favor, and with little opposition.

The three are the ones which need the attention, the thought, the zeal, the labors, the force, of a combined army of intelligent, earnest patriots.

THE END.

www.ingramcontent.com/pod-product-compliance
Lightning Source LLC
Chambersburg PA
CBHW030315270326
41926CB00010B/1373